SMART S[illegible]
Handb[illegible]

MW01658123

TURNING ON SMART POWER

Jacqueline Frischknecht, Ph.D.
and
EllaMarie Schroeder

Pieces of Learning

© 2006 Pieces of Learning
CLC0395
ISBN 1-880505-02-9

Jacqueline Frischknecht, Ph.D.

Jackie has lived in Colorado for many years. She has a B.S. in Education, an M.S. in Library Science, and a Ph.D. in Speech Communication. Her life has been defined by a consuming interest in education and in how people learn. Widowed, she has three daughters and four grandchildren. Currently she is continuing her research, writing, tutoring graduate students at the University of Colorado, and is active on the Boulder/ Dushanbe Sister Cities Association Board of Directors. She especially loves reading, music, ballet, and travel.

EllaMarie Schroeder

EllaMarie grew up in Colorado, attended college in Pennsylvania, then lived and taught in California for seventeen years. She has a B.A. in Education and an M.A. in Special Education (Gifted). Currently, she lives in Midland, Michigan, with her husband, dog, and, during college vacations, twin sons. Besides writing, she teaches part-time at a nature center. She loves hiking and canoeing, as well as sharing a love of reading, music, and travel with Jackie.

TABLE OF CONTENTS

CHAPTER	PAGE
1 READ THE DIRECTIONS	5
2 STUDY *SMART*ER & FASTER	15
3 SWITCH ON ATTITUDE POWER	33
4 CUT THROUGH DISTRACTION STATIC	47
5 CHARGE YOUR MEMORY BATTERY	74
6 FLIP THE SWITCH FOR HIGH-POWERED HABITS	112
7 PLUG IN HYPER-SPEED STUDY SKILLS	140
8 TURN ON THE MUSIC	171
INDEX	188

ACKNOWLEDGEMENTS

We wish first to thank all of our many students who helped us become very aware of how much more educators could do to teach students how to learn and maximize learning styles. Because of them we became interested in learning how to learn.

We owe a big thank you to Glenn Capelli of the True Learning Centre, Perth, Australia, for his many insights about learning and for specific ideas cited in the text.

Our family members – Larry, Chris, and Jeff Schroeder, Amalie Frischknecht, and Michael Wanke – are all owed a thank you for content suggestions and for help with formatting problems.

Friends also gave suggestions and help. So thank you to Ron Broome for for-matting help, to Kathy Ulyatt and Anne Burkholder for answering computer research questions, and to the ACI Writer's Group for general feedback.

This series truly benefited from the help of many people, so if we've forgotten anyone, we apologize. If we've made mistakes, they are ours.

CHAPTER 1
READ THE DIRECTIONS

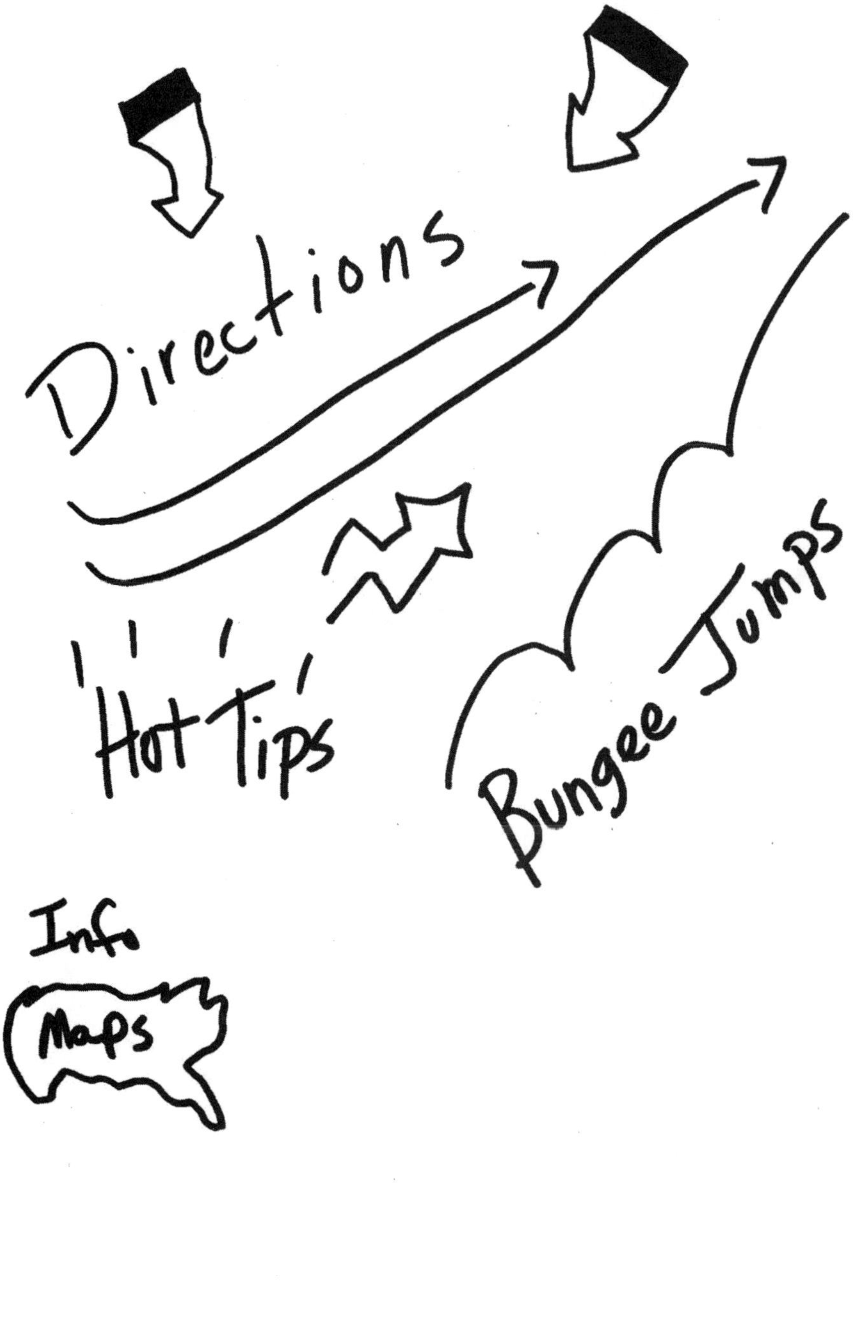

IN THIS CHAPTER

	PAGE
▶ HOW TO USE THIS HANDBOOK	8
▶ HOT TIPS	8
▶ MENTAL BUNGEE JUMPS	9
▶ A GUARANTEE	14

Sneak Previews

(This is not your ordinary handbook.)

There are many ways to read this handbook.

Don't miss the HOT TIPS.

Mental Bungee Jumping is exercise for your brain.

WARNING

Skip the next few pages
at your own risk!

Ignore them,
and it will take you much longer
to figure out the quickest way
to easily use this handbook.

HOW TO USE THIS HANDBOOK

To get a general idea of what this book is all about,

Check out the –

INFORMATION MAPS

and the

Sneak Previews

at the beginning of each chapter.

OR, You Could

flip through the entire handbook, just reading the –

HOT TIPS

These are scattered throughout the handbook.
They're food for thought
and serve as your guide to the important concepts.

Be sure to notice the pencils: ✏

They give specific directions

on how to do something.

Be sure to notice the triangles: ▶

They indicate a point to pay special attention to.

AND, maybe best of all, take a –

Mental Bungee JUMP

You've heard of bungee jumping –

it's a great way to plunge

into the unknown.

Bungee Jumping allows you to leap off tall buildings

while remaining safely anchored to your own reality

(even if you do wind up hanging by a proverbial thread!).

Mental Bungee JUMPING

is a wonderful way to take an

intellectual plunge.

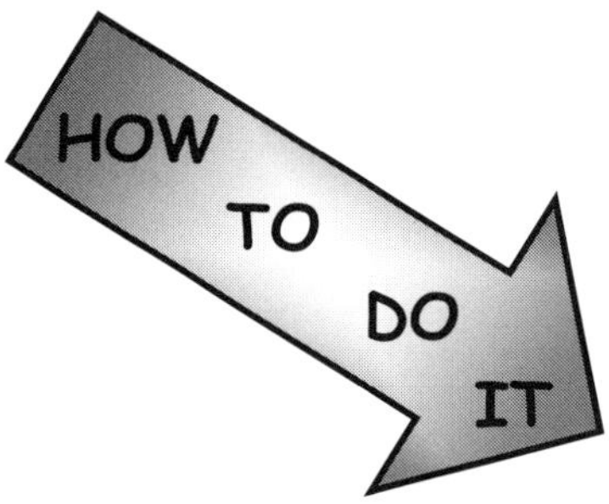

1. Suppose you're reading about how to develop a powerful memory by using all of your *SMARTS*.

2. Visualize elastic bridges stretching between all the subjects of this handbook and possibly into handbooks 2 or 3.

3. Jump on the mental bridge, grab a mental bungee cord, and bounce to the appropriate place in the handbook.

Go ahead. Give it a try right now!

Mental Bungee JUMP
To the
Many Kinds of ***SMARTS*** section
In Chapter 2 of this handbook

- Go to the **Many Kinds of *SMARTS*** information and find the Bungee Jump.
  - Follow the directions in the Mental Bungee Jump box.
    - And jump – go ahead and do it.

CONGRATULATIONS!

You have successfully made a

Mental Bungee JUMP

The Point Is:

You don't need to read this handbook in any particular order.

You can

Bungee JUMP

in any and all directions.

You can go forward,

drawkcab (backward),

sideways –

Whatever works for *YOU*.

No matter *how* people learn, nearly everyone learns best through the use of color. Since this handbook is printed in black and white, we

STRONGLY RECOMMEND ADDING

✏ **COLOR!**

✏ **COLOR!**

✏ **COLOR!**

Use colored pencils, markers, highlighters, crayons – whatever works – to draw attention to…

Headings

Sub-Headings

Mental Bungee JUMPS

V.I.P. – Very Important Points

HOT TIPS

ARROWS

and GRAPHICS of all kinds.

Using color throughout this handbook will help you remember what you read faster and for longer. It will help you become a ***SMART*** LEARNER because you will more actively engage your **Visual *SMARTS*** intelligence while also using your **Body *SMARTS*** intelligence.

V.I.P.
Very Important Point

Actively use MORE of your *SMARTS* to learn more quickly and easily.

A GUARANTEE

Last, but most important of all –

SMART STUDYING MEANS USING
ALL YOUR ***SMARTS***
TO STUDY FASTER AND BETTER!

The end result IS GUARANTEED:

YOU

POWER

UP

YOUR

GRADES!

CHAPTER 2

STUDY *SMART*ER AND FASTER

"Learning is the greatest game in life and the most fun."
Glenn Doman

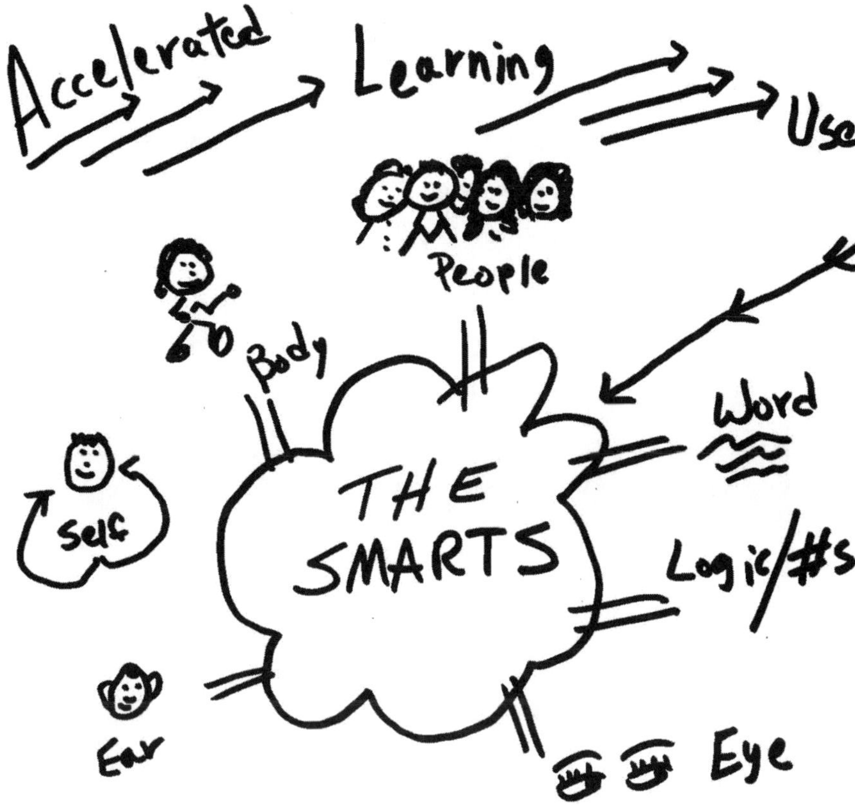

IN THIS CHAPTER

	Page
▶ SPEED UP YOUR LEARNING	17
▶ MANY KINDS OF *SMARTS*	19
▶ USING YOUR MANY *SMARTS*	28
▶ THE FINISH LINE – CELEBRATE	31

Sneak Previews

There are MANY ways to learn.
(You're ***SMART***
in more ways than one!)

There are MANY kinds of POWER.
(You have it; you can increase it;
you can use it.)

You can study (and learn) faster
and better.

Using your ***SMARTS*** will help you
make the grade.

SPEED UP YOUR LEARNING

The Bad News:

Homework and studying are inevitable.

So are tests and grades.

The Good News:

They don't have to be painful – you have the power to make them easy, fun, and fast.

Some things – like math or history or German – just take way too long to learn.

- Find out how you learn.
    - There are many ways to do it.
        - And some of them will kick your studying m.p.h. up to hyper-speed.

HOT TIP

Faster may be better – but you have to slow down long enough to learn how to power up your SMARTS.

HOT TIP

Don't ask yourself, "Am I smart?"
Instead, ask yourself, "How am I smart?"

WHAT KIND OF SMART? QUESTIONNAIRE *

DIRECTIONS: Read through all the categories (**WS, L/Ns**, etc.), mentally answering the questions. Note which ones you have more 'yes' answers for. Try to identify your top two categories.

___**WS**—Do you like to read? Are word puzzles a challenge? Do you enjoy working with words? Do you like to write?

___**L/NS**—Do you like number games? Are logic problems fun? Are you most comfortable working in a logical, orderly manner? Do you tend to consider questions in a one, two, three sequence rather than skipping around?

___**EYS**—Do you like to watch movies, television? Do you enjoy museums? Do you usually draw pictures to help you see how things look or to help you understand a concept?

___**EAS**—Do you remember what you hear? Do you like to listen to music? Do you enjoy playing a musical instrument? Do you belong to a choir?

___**BS**—Do you enjoy working with your hands, manipulating objects? Is it fun to work on your car, repair the toaster, knit, or crochet?

___**PS—**Do you like to talk things over with others? Do you have fun exploring ideas in a group? Do you shine in group discussions?

___**SS**—Do you like to think over ideas inside your head? Do you prefer to be alone to consider problems, challenges?

___**NS—**Do you like to classify objects, people, events, and/or group things into lists?

* Based on Howard Gardner's Multiple Intelligences Theory

✏ To learn more about YOUR 'smartest' ***SMARTS***, match the letters from the questionnaire **(WS, L/NS, EYS, EAS, BS, PS, SS, and NS)** to the following descriptions.

WS—WORD *SMART*

If you're **Word *SMART***, you learn best by reading or writing about a subject. And you're lucky, because **Word *SMARTS*** – reading and writing – make up one of the two intelligences most valued. **Logic/Number *SMART*** is the other.

Synonyms, antonyms,
words, words, WORDS –
The fifth dimensional travel plan!
They give ideas transportation
From my mind to conversation.*

* Schroeder & Frischknecht. *Trapped in the Tengu's Garden*

L/NS—LOGIC/NUMBER *SMART*

Your intelligence is made up of logic, order, sequence, and critical thinking if **Logical/number *SMARTS*** is your best learning style. You naturally recognize abstract patterns, organize, categorize, and use numbers and inductive and deductive reasoning. If you're interested in learning some specific ways to improve your reading, writing, and number skills –

Mental Bungee JUMP
To
Chapter 7 in this handbook
And Chapters 2 and 4
In ***SMART*** Studying Handbook 2 –
Using Your Power Base

EYS—EYE *SMART*

Do you think in pictures? 

Can you turn your mental pictures upside down  and sideways  without moving your head? Can you rotate them any which way like a draw program on a computer? Can you look at a flat map and visualize a three-dimensional road system? Can you learn from watching demonstrations? Is 'doodling'  one of your favorite pastimes (even if you 'can't draw')? You're probably **Eye *SMART***. Have you ever tried visual note taking and information mapping? If not, now would be a good time to check it out.

Mental Bungee JUMP
To
Chapter 3 in
SMART Studying Handbook 2 –
Using Your Power Base

EAS—EAR *SMART*

If you've got **Ear *SMARTS***, remembering what you hear in class is no problem at all. You probably learn foreign languages easily. And you'll most easily recall information that's presented in a rhythmic manner, because you tend to think in sounds, rhythms, and patterns. Try singing what you need to learn.

BS—BODY *SMART*

You're blessed with muscle memory if you're **Body *SMART*.**

Your body instinctively remembers a dance step or how to shoot a ball into the basket. You NEED to *move,* to be up and doing. Hands-on experiments work better for you than reading about experiments. Role-playing is another strategy that will help you learn.

PS—PEOPLE *SMART*

Do you have trouble in school because you "talk too much?" That's typical of **People-*SMART*** people. You need to talk to learn easily! You study best in groups – participating in discussions and asking questions when you're unsure. If you are **People *SMART***, you learn well by teaching what you know to others.

SS—SELF *SMART*

Do you prefer to learn by yourself? Do you shy away from team activities? Do you have a strong need for private space and alone time? You're probably a reflective learner. Your most effective learning strategy is to sit quietly, thinking about a subject or solving a problem on your own.

NS—NATURALIST *SMART* ❀❀❀

❀❀❀ Do you love being outdoors? Can you tell one kind of grass from another or identify a bird on the wing? Maybe you aren't all that interested in birds, but you're never in doubt as to what kind of car just sped by you on the freeway. An effective learning strategy for you is to classify information. ❀❀❀

No matter what kind of *SMART* you are,

the point is, YOU HAVE *SMARTS!*

And *SMARTS* are the most important kind of learning power.

PULLING YOUR SMARTS TOGETHER

Story

When Callen* was sixteen years old, his teachers assessed him as having poor short- and long-term recall.

Reading was a challenge for him; his skills could be considered passable, at best. He did, however, have a very high retention of anything musical. He sang in a choir and a rock band, and was a classically trained singer (singing in four languages, including Latin).

*A student of Glenn Capelli's at the True Learning Centre in Perth, Australia

Glenn realized Callen didn't have a memory problem. He was **Ear *SMART*** – so he needed to find a chemistry teacher who would sing to him!

He even started to record lots of his homework in rhythms and songs, which made it much easier for him to remember the things he was studying. Glenn found that Callen was also **People *SMART*** and **Body *SMART*.**

These discoveries allowed him to work with his strengths, rather than floundering with reading.

And all that time, he'd thought he was dumb!

HOT TIP

It's not what you do,
it's the way that you do it.
That's what gets results.

Callen knew he wasn't doing well in school. What he learned was that he had the power to do something about it, and it didn't necessarily mean he had to 'study' six hours a day. He learned to use his ***SMARTS*** in new ways. Over time, he

- **recognized** and **learned to use** his ***SMART* power** and
- **improved** his **grades,** practically without even trying!

You can do the same.

USING YOUR MANY SMARTS

READY —

Take a moment (or two or three or five) to ask yourself what you already know about what you're getting ready to study.

Why?

Because it's hard to add new information to something you don't even remember.

So?

Remember the saying about not being able to see the forest for the trees? Well, getting an idea of the big picture makes it much easier to organize and fit in new details.

Translated to studying, 'getting the big picture' will save you time and help you gain a better grasp of the subject.

GET SET —

Now it's time to get more actively involved. That might mean

- reorganizing ideas and or quantifying information. (**Logic/Number *SMART***)
- explaining something to someone else. (**People *SMART***)
- thinking things through from a different perspective. (**Self *SMART***)
- drawing or making lists. (**Eye *SMART***)
- classifying information. (**Naturalist *SMART***)
- singing or dancing. (**Body *SMART***)

In other words, you need to use all your SMARTS!

GO!

FREE ADVICE – TOO GOOD TO IGNORE

Review as you study.

(**Self *SMART*** – and others, depending on the method you choose.)

No, it's not. It's a good investment.

V.I.P.
Very Important Point

Information and knowledge are valuable – they're like money in the bank.

If you don't check on your deposits – make sure your account is current and accurate, and move funds from account to account as needed – you can lose money.

Likewise, if you don't check on what you've learned – review frequently – you can lose knowledge. Repeated reviewing guarantees your investment in learning is current and protected.

THE FINISH LINE – CELEBRATE!

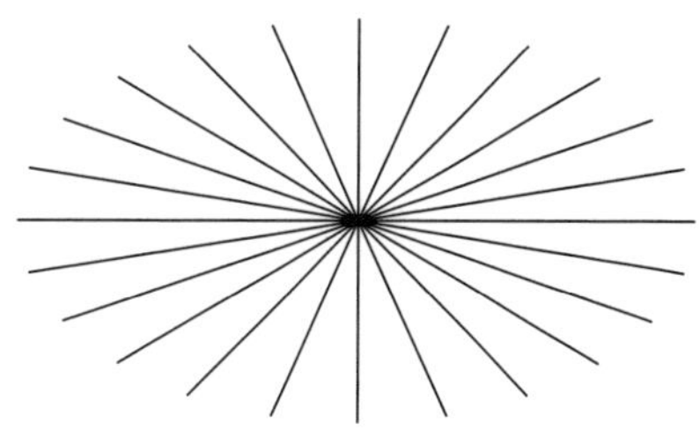

No...Celebrate your progress and your learning.

Celebration is like the period at the end of a sentence – until the period is there, the sentence isn't finished.

Celebration doesn't have to be a big deal –
it can be, but it doesn't have to be.

You can just say to yourself, "I'm done! Using my SMARTS (and my power) will mean I get better!"

If you feel celebration is truly a waste of time, consider it as therapy.

HOT TIP

A day without celebrating is like a day without chocolate.

CHAPTER 3

SWITCH ON ATTITUDE POWER

IN THIS CHAPTER

PAGE

- ATTITUDE 35
- KAIZEN 37
- SELF-TALK 40
- LUMPY PANCAKES 44
- LISTENING VERSUS HEARING 45

Sneak Previews

There are MANY ways to learn –
and ATTITUDE
is the key to all of them.

Kaizen is a special attitude.

Mistakes = lumpy pancakes.

The way you talk to yourself
can change how you act.

When you listen actively,
you use more than your ears.

ATTITUDE

Your attitude affects your grades.

I'm sick of hearing about my attitude!

But the important part is YOU are the one who's in charge of your attitudes – and that's good news!

Positive attitudes create **positive** results.

It's that **simple.**

Negative attitudes are **barriers** to success.

Negativity **cripples** your ability to think clearly and **diminishes** your capacity to learn.

HOT TIP

Attitude is more important than aptitude.

KAIZEN*

- pronounced 'KY' as in 'kayak'; 'Zen' rhymes with 'hen'

Gesundheit! Bless you!

No, no – that wasn't a sneeze – it's 'Kaizen,' a Japanese word meaning . . .

. . . the most useful positive attitude you can develop.

Kaizen translates into English as a phrase -

'to seek continuous, small,

on-going improvements.

The idea can be illustrated
through the old story about a frog in some hot water.

Story

There's a story about two frogs, two pans of water, and a biology experiment. Frog Number One swam in a pan of water. A student slowly added hot water to the pan, a little at a time. The water temperature changed slowly – from cold to cool, cool to warm, warm to hot, and finally from hot to boiling. The frog didn't react – a frog's skin isn't sensitive enough to feel gradual change. And so, it cooked.

Frog Number Two swam in the other pan of water. The student added boiling water all at once to this pan. The frog reacted instantly and quickly leapt to safety.

This probably isn't a true story – but don't experiment to find out!

However, neuroscientists say your brain indeed behaves a lot like a frog. Just like the second frog, you'll react to sudden, large, and urgent changes. But **you** would be better off learning to react to gradual, small changes; learning to be satisfied with steady progress, even if it's slow.

Using Kaizen is ***SMART***. It gives you the power to change the way you approach studying and learning.

HOT TIP

Kaizen is an attitude
That will get results.

Think of it this way –

- Attitudes are habits.
  - And you CAN control your habits.

The fine print: It's true; habits are sometimes hard to control. But with concentration, you can do it.

More fine print: It's true. You do have to go through life with brown eyes or being 5'2" tall – those are *attributes* you can't change. But you CAN change your habits – your *attitudes*.

How you talk to yourself

can improve your grades.

I don't talk to myself!

Sure you do. Everybody does.

But you might want to think about which 'voice' you use...

Huh?

Everyone has three main voices:*

- The **YES** voice.
- The *I DON'T KNOW* voice.
- The **NO** voice.

The different voices speak to you in typical ways:

'YES' VOICE	*'I DON'T KNOW' VOICE*	'NO' VOICE
I can do it.	*Maybe I'll get it done.*	**I can't do it.**
I **have the** necessary **abilities.**	*I'm not sure if I can.*	**I'm no good.**
I can **get help** from somebody.	*I'll wait till someone asks me.*	**I'm dumb.**
I'll **do it now**.	*I'll do it later.*	**It's your fault.**
This is a **challenge**.	*This is boring.*	**This is useless.**
There's always **an alternative**.	*I've got an excuse.*	**It's too hard.**
		I'm too little.
		Who cares, anyway?

*based on conversations with Glenn Capelli of the True Learning Centre, Perth, Australia

Many people use their **NO** voice most often
and their **YES** voice least, especially
when talking about school stuff. But –

V.I.P.
Very Important Point

Your brain listens to you.
What you *say* changes
how you *think*.

And what you think changes how you act – (**Self *SMARTS*** *in action!*)

That's amazing! Words are really powerful!

If you tell yourself you can't understand algebra...you're probably right.

But (put your **Word *SMARTS*** to work) if you tell yourself, *"It'll be tough, but I can probably, someday) understand Algebra,"* you'll be more likely to stick with it, and chances Are you'll surprise yourself and actually get it.

*But I **DON'T** understand it!*

Don't be your own worst enemy. Maybe you don't understand...but maybe you just made a mistake (or two or ten).

HOT TIP

Mistakes are just lumpy pancakes –
maybe not perfect, but edible,
not irretrievable disasters.

LUMPY PANCAKES*

* Based on the work of Glenn Capelli, True Learning Centre, Perth, Australia

Do you ever make pancakes? Are they ever lumpy?

Nobody much likes lumpy pancakes.

So what do you do with them?

EllaMarie feeds them to her dog, Pepper, who absolutely loves them.

If you made lumpy pancakes, you wouldn't waste much time moaning and groaning about it – it's not that important. Likewise, you wouldn't bother trying to hide, deny, blame someone else, or lie about it.

You'd probably just laugh, feed them to the dog, and try to figure out how to make tastier pancakes next time. Or you might switch to waffles.

▶ The **same** should go for other kinds of mistakes – **especially school-related ones.**

If you pay no more mind to mistakes at school than you would to lumpy pancakes at home, your studying will progress more smoothly.

Joke of the day: *How are algebra class and breakfast the same?*

Answer: *You can have lumpy pancakes in both.*

LISTENING VERSUS HEARING

Hearing is something you do with your ears (assuming they're normally functional). Listening is done with your mind. (It still counts as **Ear *SMARTS***.)

Listening is an attitude.

Listening – not *hearing.*

There's a huge difference between hearing and listening.

Here's the scoop!

- People can't talk as fast as you can think, so there's plenty of time for you to **become actively involved** – truly 'listening' instead of just 'hearing.'

  - Mentally **question** what has been said.
    - **Make a note** of what you don't understand.
      - Deliberately **think about** what you hear.

It's Easy.

- **Learn your teacher's typical lecture format and listen for it.**
  Most lectures contain an introduction, a thesis statement (the topic), the body (information to be learned), and a summary. There may also be stories, jokes, examples, visual aids, and demonstrations.

- **Be on the alert for possible test questions.**
  Take special note of such phrases as –

  'an important conclusion…'

  'a principal reason for…'

  'the underlying theme…'

  'this basic idea…'

HOT TIP

You can DECIDE to become a better listener.

CHAPTER 4

CUT THROUGH DISTRACTION STATIC

IN THIS CHAPTER

	PAGE
▶ FOCUS ABILITY	49
▶ DISTRACTIONS	53
▶ CONCENTRATION QUICK FIXES	72

Sneak Previews

You CAN learn to focus
and concentrate!

There are lots of distractions.
There are also MANY
strategies for coping
with distractions.

Not all distractions are equal.
Some are external –
others are internal.

In an emergency,
you can use
special 9-1-1 quick-fixes.

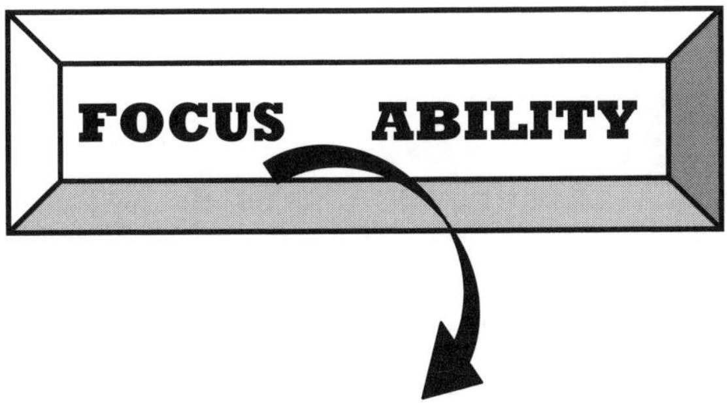

Do you have trouble concentrating even when you're really trying to pay attention?

Or maybe you just can't concentrate quite long enough? You can concentrate for 20 minutes, but class lasts 50 minutes...

OBVIOUS CONCLUSION:

If this describes you, you've got a dangerous mismatch!

Time to take ACTION!

TRACK YOUR TIME

Test

Pay attention long enough to notice how long it takes before you notice you're not paying attention in class or to what you're studying.

- If the answer is 'less than an hour,' work until you can increase your concentration time to about an hour (both for class and study time).
  - If you can easily concentrate for more than an hour, you'll do fine in class, but you may need to take a study break sooner.

Story

Jessie can literally work on a project for hours at a time. She's often surprised, when she finally looks up, to discover she's skipped lunch and maybe supper, too, without ever noticing. So she's learned to use a kitchen timer to keep track of time. Setting the timer to ring each hour means she gets up and stretches, moves around, and re-energizes. Some words of caution – Jessie also learned she needs to use a timer that's really irritating, so she's forced to get up to turn it off. That way she's sure to notice it.

If you couldn't focus long enough to figure out how long you can pay attention (or even if you could), try this questionnaire to learn more –

HOW'S YOUR FOCUS ABILITY?

See what you can learn about your ability to focus by answering the following true-false questions.
It's hard to begin, because my mind keeps jumping around.___
I seldom get everything done that I planned to in a study session. ___
If something goes wrong, it usually has a negative effect on the rest of my day. ___
When I've been distracted, I have trouble getting back to studying. ___
My concentration is easily interrupted. ___
I don't study some subjects much because they're boring. ___
I usually work on several subjects at once. ___
I don't sleep well because I'm worrying. ___
I get irritable and stressed when I am interrupted. ___
Interruptions happen a lot when I'm studying. ___

Score

7-10 True: Time for a change – it looks like you're easily distracted.

4-6 True: Not too bad. Apparently you let interruptions affect you, but on the whole you're doing a good job of maintaining focus.

0-3 True: Time to celebrate.

Are you celebrating?

Terrific!

If you're not ready to celebrate, read on. See if you can figure out what's keeping you from concentrating.

How can I concentrate on studying when birds are singing right outside my window...and the phone rings...and the weather is beautiful...

You need some distraction distractions!

HOT TIP

Learn to recognize the distractions – then you can beat them.

It's true there are a lot of distractions out there. And in there. Sometimes it feels like almost anything and everything around you hijacks your attention. Don't despair – you CAN learn to concentrate and become a powerful learner.

Start by using your Logic and your Self SMARTS* – analyze what's claiming your attention.

* **Even if these aren't your strongest *SMARTS*, you do have them, and this is a good time to use them.**

EXTERNAL DISTRACTIONS

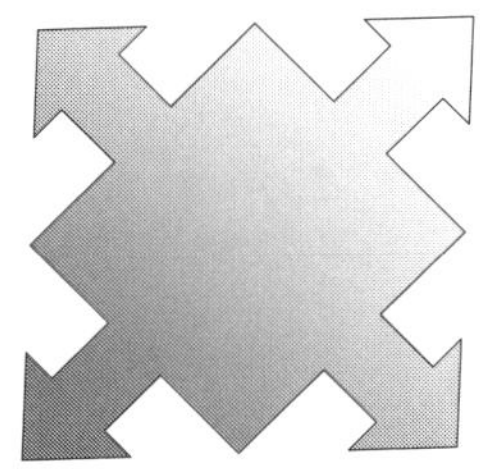

These would be the 'out there' distractions...

LOCATION

Did you know that **where** you study affects **how well** you study?

FREE ADVICE – TOO GOOD TO IGNORE

The first external distraction you should pay attention to is Location.

LOCATION DISTRACTIONS ANALYSIS

List the three places where you usually study in the order you use them most:

A ____

B ____

C ____

Now record your total of true (T) and false (F) responses to the statements below for EACH of the three places you usually study.

____ 1. Other people often interrupt me when I study here.

____ 2. Much of what I can see here reminds me of things that don't have anything to do with studying.

____3. I often hear the radio or TV when I study here.

____4. I often hear the phone ringing when I study here.

____5. I think I take too many breaks when I study here.

____6. I seem to be especially bothered by distractions here.

____7. I usually don't study here at regular times each week.

____8. My breaks tend to be too long when I study here.

____9. I tend to start conversations with people when I study here.

___10. I spend time on the phone here when I should be studying.

___11. It's uncomfortably warm or cold here.

___12. The chair, table, and lighting arrangements here are not helpful for studying.

___13. I don't like studying here.

The location with the most 'false' responses on the questionnaire is probably your best choice – least distracting.

✶Coping Strategy

- Make it a habit to **study** in your identified **'least distracting spot'** whenever possible.
- **Associate** being in that spot with studying.
- Use your **People *SMARTS*** – make sure your family and friends make the same association (That, by itself, will make distractions less frequent.)

NOISE

'Noise' = any sound that distracts you:

television…a ringing phone

slamming doors… siblings playing

birdsong…conversation at the next table

traffic outside your window

✶Coping Strategies

- Define the noises that distract you. Then **train yourself to develop selective hearing.** Use your **Ear *SMARTS***.

Selective hearing is the art of ignoring things you don't want to hear.

You may already be quite good at it – have you ever slept through your alarm clock? Or have you ever 'not heard' your mom mention the trash needed emptying?

- If your study place has a television or phone, unplug them when you're studying. If that's not possible, **wear earplugs.**

VISUAL DISTRACTIONS

Anything in your line of vision could be
a visual distraction if it's more interesting
than what you're studying:

pictures… the window…
a novel you're ½ way through…
a bag of potato chips…the comics…
a pile of computer games…

*Take out some Distraction Insurance –
Remove distractions from your study area.*

✶Coping Strategies

- Put away your computer games, candy bars, email that needs an answer – in other words, **clear your desk** of everything except your study materials. Put your **Eye *SMARTS*** to work where YOU want them!

- **If you can't move the distractions, move yourself** – face a blank wall so you can't see friends playing ultimate Frisbee – or whatever activity – right outside your window. And be double sure you can't see the fridge.

HEAVY CLASS LOAD

Too many classes this term? Too much reading? No time to get it all done?

✶Coping Strategies

- **Set up a study schedule.**
- **Study one subject at a time** for a specified time.
- To avoid boredom, **break your study sessions into chunks** and study a mix of different subjects. For more ideas –

Mental Bungee JUMP
To
Chapter 2 in
SMART Studying Handbook 3 –
Extending Your Power

INTERNAL DISTRACTIONS

Not all distractions are outside problems – some are of my own making, within my own mind...

A WANDERING MIND

You're studying, you're in class, you're even in the middle of a conversation –

You've been 1,000 miles away!

and you suddenly realize
you don't know what's just happened!

✶Coping Strategies

- **Change what you're doing** – you've been reading? Switch to writing.
- **Change what you're studying** – study biology for a while instead of Spanish; switch from history to math.
- **Get active** – read aloud, chant, sing, pace –whatever – Use your **Ear** and **Body** ***SMARTS!***

It sounds like "coping" mostly means thinking about stuff in a different way.

Thinking a little differently and then doing things a little differently can make a BIG difference.

REPEATING THOUGHTS, SONGS, JINGLES

Have you ever had a tune or an advertising jingle (or worse, an argument) repeat endlessly in your head no matter how hard you try to get rid of it? Your **Ear *SMARTS*** are out of control – how annoying! It usually doesn't do a bit of good to tell yourself you won't sing that song or re-fight that fight. The more you try to forget it, the more persistent it becomes. That's because your thoughts go where your energy goes – and all your energy is going toward the nuisance song/jingle/fight.

✶Coping Strategies

- **Tell yourself:** ***STOP***. Then firmly re-focus. Bring your attention back to wherever you want it to be. Don't waste energy trying to keep the nuisance out of your mind; instead put your energy into the command to stop.

- **Do some silly exercises** while remaining seated at your desk. Scrunch up your face, hold a moment, relax. Do it again. Pat your tummy, and rub your head. Try to wiggle your ears. Use your **Body *SMARTS*** to outwit your head! The nuisance will probably flee while you're concentrating on silly stuff.

LACK OF ACTIVITY

It's hard to continue concentrating if you're inactive for too long a period. Movement keeps both your body and your brain awake by circulating oxygen. That's especially necessary if you're an active person who really likes to be up and moving. But even if you're a couch potato, sitting in one position can wear you out.

Sitting for long study sessions qualifies as 'lack of activity' as far as your body is concerned!

I can get tired by not being active??

Time to use Body SMARTS.

✶Coping Strategies

- **Get up and move away from your desk!** Stand up and jog in place. Touch your toes a few times.

- **Get moving while sitting at your desk.** Tap your fingers on your desk. Blink your eyes; shake your head. Shift your body position, wiggle your toes, shrug your shoulders. Squeeze a Koosh ball.

LACK OF SLEEP

Have you ever fallen asleep while studying? Most people have. What about falling asleep while sitting at your computer and waking up when your head hits the monitor?

OBVIOUS TRUTH

It's impossible to concentrate if you're sleepy.

✶Coping Strategies

- **Schedule concentration-demanding activities for when you're mentally and physically fresh.** That means you need to know your own energy cycles (Use **Self *SMARTS***). For information:

Mental Bungee JUMP
To
Chapter 2:
Manage An Energy Crisis
in
SMART Studying Handbook 3 –
Extending Your Power

- **Don't sit in a comfortable armchair** or stretch out on the sofa or your bed to read.

- If no matter what you do, you're still too sleepy to concentrate, give up and go to bed. **Get up earlier the next morning** if necessary.

- If you're sleepy during the day, **take a short nap.** (Notice the word 'short.' Too long of a nap means you'll wake up groggy instead of refreshed.)

HUNGER

A growling stomach *Grrrrr!* is hard to ignore! (If you're hungry, it can be almost impossible to concentrate.) On the other hand, if you've just eaten a big meal, it's also hard to concentrate.

✶Coping Strategies

- **Be moderate** in your eating habits – not too much, not too little.
- Eat a **balanced diet**.
- **Watch** your **sugar intake.**
- **Watch** your **caffeine consumption.**

VISION PROBLEMS

Reading for a long time gives me a headache, but I can see just fine.

That almost certainly is a sign of some sort of vision problem.

It's because the words blur and jump around on the page.

Definitely a vision problem!

✶Coping Strategy

Time for an eye exam!

✏ If an eye exam doesn't reveal any problems, **consider the possibility that you may be somewhat dyslexic.** Give your **Eye *SMARTS*** a fair chance!

Mental Bungee JUMP

To

Chapter 2: the information on dyslexia in ***SMART*** Studying Handbook 2 – *Using Your Power Base*

LACK OF MOTIVATION

✶Coping Strategies

- **Study for a shorter-than-usual time.** Set yourself a challenge – "I'm going to finish Chapter 4 in the next half-hour."

✏ **Plan a reward** for when you've finished X amount of studying.

✏ **Think of ways you can use the information** (relevant information is always more interesting).

✏ **Study another subject for a while**. Then go back to the 'boring' subject.

***FREE ADVICE —
TOO GOOD TO IGNORE***

If nothing else works, try this on for size - if it's boring now, think how awful it will be the second or third time around!

Hit the fast-forward button and get into high gear!

DAY DREAMING

Are you a daydreamer?

Huh, what? Did you say something?

HOT TIP

Daydreaming and studying don't mix. Self-discipline is needed!

✶Coping Strategies

- If you catch yourself daydreaming, **re-focus** with a quick mental review.
- **Take a short break** (short means no more than five minutes).
- As a last resort, go ahead – **daydream for a bit**. Stand, facing away from your desk. (This is important – you don't want to associate your desk with your daydreams.)

Chances are you won't daydream very long – you'll get tired of standing there.

STRESS AND WORRY

NOT-SO-OBVIOUS TRUTH

Being a student is a full time, often stressful job.

But if you're feeling stressed or worried, it's hard to concentrate.

✶Coping Strategy

✏ Student stress and worry are amazingly common problems.

For help –

Mental Bungee JUMP

To
Chapter 4 in
SMART Studying Handbook 3 –
Extending Your Power

CONCENTRATION QUICK FIXES

There aren't any really good, quick,concentration fixes. But if nothing else works, try the **9-1-1 approach.**

✶ **9-1-1- Coping Strategies**

✏ **Figure out how you work best** – with a study partner, group or alone. Then try to **study that way as often as possible**.

> *Maybe concentration's not the problem. Maybe you lack necessary knowledge or understanding.*

- **Gather more information** on the subject you're studying.

- **Stop if your brain feels saturated.** Switch to a new topic. Take a short break. Quit for now, but **set a specific re-start time**.

- **Decide** –
  - **whether you fully intend** to study. If not, don't waste your time 'trying.'
  - **how long** you intend to study.
  - **how much** work you intend to accomplish.

- If you lose focus while reading, **stop at the end of each page.** Count to 10 slowly. Turn the page and continue.

- **Drink a glass of water or some herbal tea**. Remember – caffeine is not an acceptable quick fix. *(Caffeine provides a short term jolt, but then it lets you down big-time, and it's even harder to concentrate.)*

CHAPTER 5

CHARGE YOUR MEMORY BATTERY

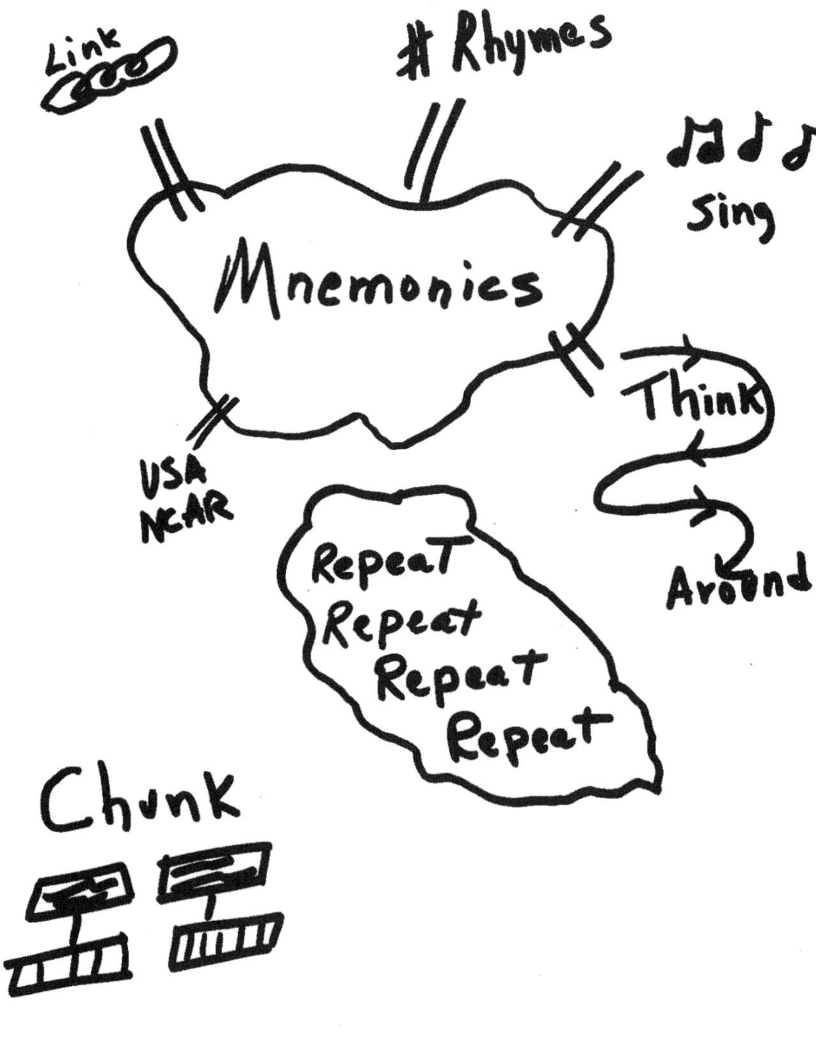

IN THIS CHAPTER

	Page
▶ OWNER'S GUIDE TO MEMORY	76
▶ HOW MEMORY WORKS	82
▶ MNEMONIC METHODS	97

Sneak Previews

There are MANY ways to remember –
YOU have a fantastic memory!

'Use it or Lose it'
is true about memory.
(And it's not 'all in your head.')

Memory comes
in more than one flavor.

Practice doesn't necessarily
make perfect...but REVIEW might.

PLAY time!
Try out memory games & methods.

Story

When she was only 5 or 6, Katie surprised her mother, saying "Do you know what I like to do – I like to walk backward through my mind."

"What do you mean?" the puzzled mother asked.

Katie's impatient answer: "Oh, you know. I like to use my remembery."

Do you like to use your remembery?

No point. I've got a bad memory.

OWNER'S GUIDE TO MEMORY*

*Yes, you are a registered memory owner!

V.I.P.
Very Important Point

You CAN'T have a 'bad' memory because your 'remembery' has a LIMITLESS capacity for holding information.

Experiments during hypnosis and brain surgery prove that every single thing that ever happens to you – and everything you have ever learned – is in there some-where.

That's not just limitless – that's almost scary!

Minor Problem:

There's **no specific location** in your brain devoted to memory storage. Memory bits are packed into a **complex network** of **over 100 billion neurons**. The number of possible inter-connections between memory-storage neurons is larger than the number of atoms in the universe – there isn't even a name for such a number!

So how am I ever supposed to find a specific memory?

That's exactly the problem.

The challenge isn't a simple case of remembering.

The challenge is in retrieving – calling up – what you know.

I'm no good at that – it's way too hard...

You need to get rid of some of your Memory Myths –

Memory Myths

1. Memory is a thing you do or don't have – and it's either good or bad.
2. There's a secret to having a good memory.
3. Remembering too much can clutter up your mind.
4. Older people have poor memories.
5. There's a right way to memorize.

Not one of them is true!

Next, recognize that there are several types of memory. And NONE of them are 'good' or 'bad'!

The two main memory types are

[‘Short term’]

– what happened earlier today

or maybe what you studied last night

and

[——‘L-o-n-g t-e-r-m’——]

– what happened longer ago than last week

Think of it like parking at the airport – will you need to get the car (or information) out of the lot in an hour or a month?

Two more types of memory (which can be either short- or long-term) are

'Recognition' – simply recognizing you've seen or heard or smelled something before.

You 'recognize' the kid at the video store, but can't remember her name.

and

'Functional' – when you can remember what you know and use it.

You can greet the kid by name.

HOT TIP

Recognition memory isn't enough.
Functional Memory is your key to success.

HOW MEMORY WORKS

Memory works

by creating links

between bits of information.

TRY THESE

MEMORY TIPS

You know that old saying –

People remember 90% of what they do, 75% of what they see, and 20% of what they hear.

BE AN ACTIVE LEARNER

Experiment...

Snuggle down comfortably in a soft chair and begin to study. Chances are your mind will wander or you'll catch yourself daydreaming or dozing. Take a break after 30 minutes (or when you wake up), and then try to remember what you studied.

Now, try sitting up straight on the edge of your desk chair. Actively work at seeing, speaking, and writing the information you want to learn. Thirty minutes later, test yourself. Did you prove the theory?

HOT TIP

To develop a powerful memory, use all of your SMARTS.

HOW TO DO IT

Mental Bungee JUMP

To

Chapter 2 in this handbook p. 15

Here are more ideas:

SEEING (**Eye** and **Naturalist *SMART***)

How do you make 'seeing' active?

Good question.

Answer: Notice details and patterns, classify differences and similarities, and 'visualize.' That means making brain pictures of what you're studying.

Staying with **words** uses the **left side** of your brain.

Visualizing gets the **right side** working.

What you learn with your

WHOLE BRAIN

stays there longer!

V.I.P.
Very Important Point

Visualization improves memory. It's especially important to create visual pictures of concepts.

But concepts are abstract...

That does make it challenging. But that's where VISUALIZATION comes in. Try this –

Visualization

Close your eyes and use your imagination. What color is the concept? What shape? What kind of symbols can you connect to the ideas and themes? Can you design a setting for the concept? Can you make it into a cartoon? Can you turn it into a chart or graph? Try making a video of it in your mind. Create an information map. Do you know what the people you're studying look like? Find out – or make it up. Remember, your brain loves to visualize.

SPEAKING (Ear *SMART*)

Add **speaking aloud** to your bag of study tricks.

It works better than simply repeating information silently inside your head. That's because it's much easier to trick your mind into thinking it knows something well than it is to trick your ears.

WRITING AND MOVING...
(**Body *SMART***)

The act of **writing something down** reinforces it in your mind. Have you ever made a list of who you want to invite to a party, then discovered when you get to school you left the list at home? Chances are you can remember almost every name anyway.

But, don't tap your pencil or click your pen – too noisy – sure to get you in trouble!

Other than writing, **moving** much in a classroom is hard, but if you're a **Body *SMART*** person, even rhythmically tapping your finger on your knee will help you remember information. But when you study, be sure to **move** – squeeze a ball, pace, or dance while you chant your lessons. In other words –

MOVE!

❖❖❖❖ REPETITION ❖❖❖❖ REPETITION ❖❖❖❖ REPETITION ❖❖❖❖ ❖❖❖❖ REPETITION ❖❖❖❖

(All *SMARTS*)

Do you remember learning to play a musical instrument or ride a bike? How did you do it? You **practiced** and **practiced** – **repeated** and **repeated**. Repetition is one of the most commonly used memory techniques.

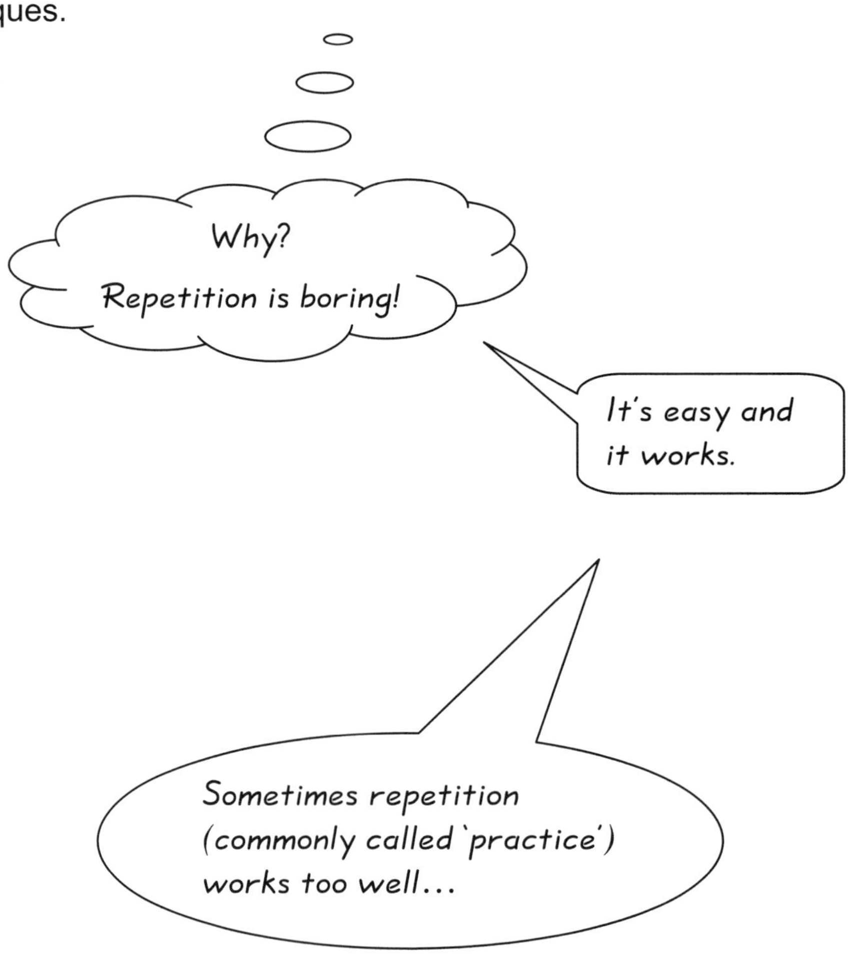

V.I.P.
Very Important Point

Practice does not necessarily make perfect.
Incorrect practice makes disaster!

Be careful when learning new knowledge and new habits. Concentrate on **getting it right** and **practicing correctly**. Learning something and then un-learning it is triple work. Breaking a bad habit takes much more effort than learning it right in the first place.

Yeah...I worked hard at not 'throwing like a girl,' but when I went out for softball at school, the coach made me learn to throw all over again! It was awful!

HOT TIP

CORRECT PRACTICE makes PROGRESS!

Note: Practice doesn't last forever.

Story

On a vacation, the Conrad family decided to rent bikes and go for a ride. Dad got on a bike and took off across the grassy meadow path. The ten year old got on a bike, and off she went. Mom got on a bike and promptly fell off. She tried again and again and kept falling off. It had been years since Mom had ridden a bike and she'd apparently forgotten how.

That's crazy – nobody forgets how to ride a bike!

Mom Conrad did. Listen to the rest of the story...

The Story . . . continued

As Mom was showing off her bruises that night, her small daughter solemnly announced she knew why her mom had fallen. Curious, the mom asked why. "Well," came the reply, "your center of gravity must have shifted."

As father and mother collapsed in laughter, Mom could only stammer, "Maybe so." One thing was painfully clear – her bike-riding practice was sadly out of date!

USE ASSOCIATION

Sometimes association – a way of tying ideas together – works more quickly than repetition or memorization. Suppose you have to remember a long number: 11,624,935. There's nothing particularly interesting about that number except the fact that you've been assigned to remember it. How will you do it?

Think of it in terms of price: $116, 249. 35. What could you do with that much money . . .?

Or think in terms of time – 11:04:23 (the time the plane leaves on the great vacation you're taking with your $116, 249.35). Or distance – 110,423 miles (how far you can go with your money).

Or suppose you need to remember dates for a history test. Here's an example of how a more complex association works:

Quick –

what's the date of the Norman invasion of England?

Facts:
The Norman invasion happened in 1066. The Normans were French. They defeated the Anglo-Saxons, bringing a centralized form of feudalism, and therefore, a powerful king, civil peace, and relative personal security to England.

Create pictures in your mind.

Associations:
There are ten letters in "Anglo-Saxon" and six letters in both "Norman" and "French"—10-66. Now imagine a disgusted ten-year-old harassed by six-year-old twins who gleefully chant "London Bridge Is Falling Down" all afternoon.

Ask yourself what does this idea remind me of? How is it similar to something I already know? How is it different?

The more you can link the new information into what you already know, the more meaning it will have for you.

Association Links:
I have twin sons who, when they were younger, were fascinated with knights and armor and the trappings of feudalism. I've witnessed many a mock battle, complete with repetitive chants and noisy teasing. I'm also familiar with older siblings' disgust with younger siblings' games. It's all a bit different from the civil peace the Normans brought to England! (Links work whether they're similarities or differences.)

When you're creating associations, use the

'Law of Vividness'

Make the associations as colorful and vivid as possible. **Exaggerate. Animate. Include sound, odors, and color.** The more unusual you make the picture, the more powerful it will be and the more likely you are to remember it.

Sounds like a lot of trouble. Why should I do all that?

Think about a time when you had a big fight with your best friend. Do you remember what happened the day before the fight?

No, why would I?

Exactly! You have no reason to remember the ordinary day before. But you do remember the fight – that was an extraordinary event.

And that's why you need to use the 'Law of Vividness' in your studying.

Note: It may take a little longer to learn this way – especially if the process is a new to you.

But if you simply memorize for a test, chances are you'll have to do it all over again for a mid-term and/or final.

So putting in the extra effort up front

will actually save you time.

PRACTICE OVER-LEARNING

JOKE of the DAY:
Study enough to learn more than you think you need to know.

Ha, ha!
Very funny.

Second JOKE of the DAY:
The 'JOKE' wasn't really a joke.

If you know a whole lot about something, you're more likely to recall the specific bit of information you need when you need it.

LEARN TO 'CHUNK'

Think of your short-term memory as a small purse that can hold seven coins. If the coins are pennies, then the purse can only hold seven cents. But if the coins are nickels (each representing a chunk of five pennies), the purse can hold 35 cents. If they're dimes, the capacity is increased to 70 cents. Quarters up the capacity to $1.75, and using Sacajawea dollars would mean the purse could hold $7.00 – quite an increase over seven cents!

It doesn't matter

whether you put

lots of information

or a little bit of information

into each chunk

What matters is dividing

the information into chunks.

Count them.

Seven chunks is the limit.

HOT TIP

Information organized into no more than seven chunks is easier to recall.

MNEMONIC METHODS

A mnemonic (pronounced: ni-MAHN-ik) is a formula or rhyme used to help you remember something complex.

Like – 'Thirty days hath September, April, June, and November.

The word 'mnemonic' comes from the name of the Greek goddess of memory. So in a way, these devices come straight from the gods – which means they're not only bound to work, they're powerful!

Mnemonics work sort of like a computer search engine. You code the memory you need to find. The mnemonic tells you

- ▶ where to locate the first item,
  - ▶ how to get from one item to the next, and
    - ▶ how to know when you've reached the last item.

There are lots of types of mnemonics. Some may work better for you than others.

In fact, some might not work at all – for you.

That's OK – different people have different styles. Experiment!

Here are some general guidelines
to get you started
in making up your own mnemonics.

Use LOTS of your
SMARTS.

- Make your mnemonic clearly **related** to what you want to remember.
- Involve as many **senses** as possible.
- Create **colorful, three-dimensional** mental images.
- Then add **sound, rhythm, movement, touch and scent**.
- **Exaggerate the size** of the important parts of your image.
- Use **humor**.
- Put the mnemonic in **list form**, with numbers or symbols, or some other way of remembering the order.
- **Keep it simple.**

Try some specific types of mnemonics –

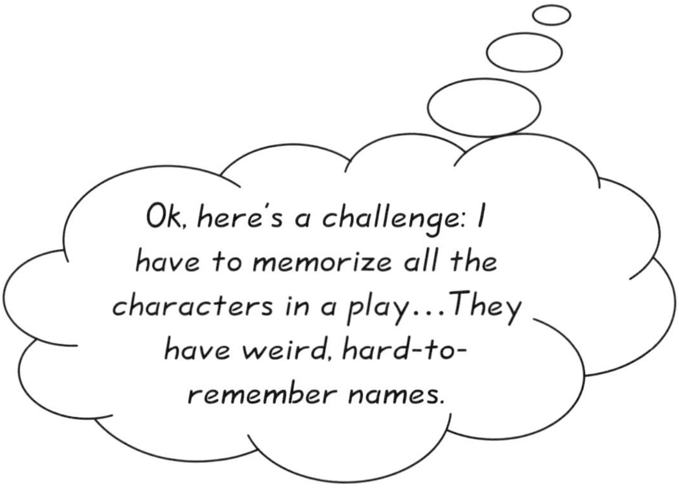

Time to think about using:

ALPHABETIZING LISTS

(**Naturalist *SMART***– cataloging items into a list,
Word *SMART* – alphabetizing)

- First, list the characters in alphabetical order. See if that makes it easy to remember.
  - If that doesn't help, rearrange until you can make up a sentence using the first letter in each name (see ACROSTICS, page 102).

Character List*:
Antonio
Curio
Fabian
Feste
Orsino
Malvolio
Maria
Olivia
Sir Toby Belch
Sir Andrew Aguecheek
Valentine
Viola

* Shakespeare, Twelfth Night

Mnemonic:
A Collection **F**airly
Full **O**f **M**any
Miserable **O**lives, **S**o
Some **V**ictims **V**omit.

It doesn't paint a pretty picture, but it's memorable! (You could probably make up a better one.)

HOT TIP

Mnemonics work best for learning/remembering lists or details or 'stuff' in a specific order.

ACRONYMS (Word *SMART*)

Acronyms are WORDS created from the first letters in a series of words.

For example, it's easier to remember 'Laser' than 'light amplification by stimulated emission of radiation.'

When you were in elementary school did you use 'HOMES' to remember the Great Lakes?

Huron
Ontario
Michigan
Erie
Superior

ACROSTICS (Word *SMART*)

Acrostics are similar to acronyms,
but they're **SENTENCES** instead of words.

You mean like,
"Every Good Boy
Does Fine"?

Exactly. And I bet
that's proof you know
the notes on the lines
of the treble clef are
"E, G, B, D, F."

HOT TIP

Acronyms and acrostics allow
the first letter of each word
to trigger your memory
of the rest of the information.

THINKING AROUND IT
(Logic *SMART*)

'Thinking Around It' means to reconstruct your thoughts or movements **STEP-BY-STEP** to help you remember something.

I lost my keys and had to leave the car at school and get a ride home...I don't even want to think about it!

Give this a try. Think back to when you last had them... maybe you can "see" where you left them.

If that doesn't work, think about what you've done since you last had your keys –

I walked into school, said 'hi' to Amanda, went to my locker...

Eventually you'll remember where your keys are.

Other information can be recovered the same way.

When talking with someone, and being interrupted, have you ever had to ask: "What was I saying?" By re-constructing the general content of your conversation, you can usually remember what else you wanted to say.

CHANTS, RAPS, AND SONGS
(Primarily **Ear *SMART***)

Chants, raps, and songs use tune and rhythm.

You can make up a song, rap, or chant to help you remember almost anything.

Everybody knows –

'In fourteen hundred and ninety-two,
Columbus sailed the ocean blue.'

Or what about the 'A, B, C ' song? It's still popular on Sesame Street.

I'd feel dumb singing the A,B,Cs. Anyway, I can't sing.

Use any song you want – 'Yankee Doodle' or the latest hit. Make up your own words, using chemistry or math or history facts. And it doesn't matter a bit if you sing well – it's the silly words that count!

LINK AND STORY
(Primarily **Word *SMART***)

Items are connected in a story in the Link and Story Method.

My mom's going to say making up stories doesn't quite sound like studying!

But she'll be wrong. Making up a story is a great way to remember any information that can be put into a list.

Advantages:
Stories are easier – and lots more fun – to remember than lists.

Disadvantages:
Stories take longer to create than lists.

HOW TO DO IT

Make your list. Turn the items into pictures in your mind. Follow the mnemonics rules – make your pictures memorable, colorful, silly, and active. Imagine you need to remember a birthday list. It begins with –

books
sweaters
sled...

You might create a story something like the following:

Possible Story...

It was a cold and snowy day. A group of books decided to have a holiday in the mountains. Dressed in brightly colored ski sweaters, they gathered at the top of the pass. Several books jumped on their sleds and flew down the mountain. Unfortunately, half way down...

Well, you finish!

NUMBER/RHYME
(Logic/Number *SMARTS*)

The Number/Rhyme Method is a simple way to remember lists in a specific order.

> *List the facts you need to remember, then link them to numbers – like 'One-two-buckle-my-shoe.'*

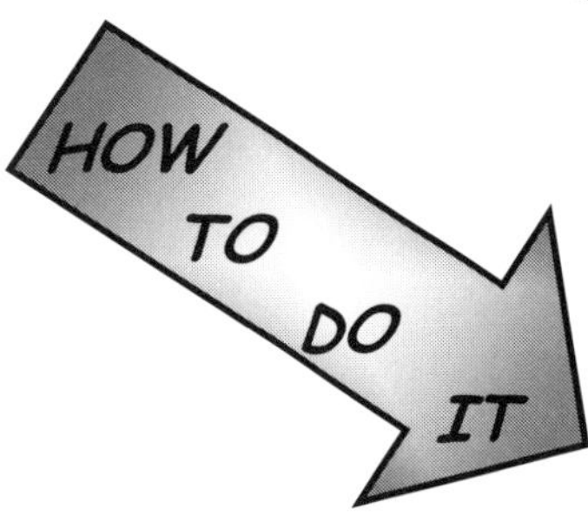

Back to your birthday list. Remember, you need –

books, sweaters, and a sled

- Start with a rhyming scheme. It's useful to use the same scheme each time. That way, you don't have to waste energy remembering the rhymes as well as your list. You can make up your own, but here's an example:

1 = BUN	6 = STICKS
2 = SHOE	7 = HEAVEN
3 = TREE	8 = GATE
4 = DOOR	9 = WINE
5 = HIVE	10 = HEN

✏ Now link your list to the rhymes. For example:

1 = BUN = books.

Visualize a pile of books dumped in a shopping cart.

2 = SHOE = sweaters.

Visualize brightly colored sweaters swirling around the store in a mad dance.

3 = TREE = a sled.

As you make your way through the store the sweaters jig and jog toward the shopping cart. Each sweater swoops down and wraps itself around a book, rushes to a sled, and plops down.

Got the idea?

The familiar scheme and the silliness help you remember your list. So do the numbers.

You'll immediately know if you've missed an item, because there will be holes in the number sequence.

BUT – DO MNEMONICS WORK?

Yes.

IF – and it's an important 'if' – they're learned and used properly.

And once you learn a system, you can use it for lots of different memorization tasks.

But there are drawbacks.

Mnemonic methods won't help you understand information, and they don't aid the critical thinking process. Another drawback is they can take a lot of time and be complicated to learn. If you don't enjoy games, learning to use mnemonics may not be for you.

Mnemonics clearly work well for **Word *SMART*** and **Logic/Number *SMART*** people, because they deal with words and keeping things in order. **Naturalist *SMART*** learners use classification type mnemonics easily. If some of the other ***SMARTS*** work better for you, you may need to modify your techniques, depending on your learning style. Are you an **Ear *SMART*** learner? Always *include sound cues* in the mnemonics you use. If you're a **Body *SMART*** learner – *add actions* to your mnemonics. If you're **Eye *SMART***, of course you'd ***add pictures.*** If you're **People *SMART***, you'll want to ***share*** your mnemonics with your friends, but if you're **Self *SMART***, you may want to ***keep it private.***

HOT TIP

Mnemonic methods work well with rote memorization.

CHAPTER 6

FLIP THE SWITCH FOR HIGH-POWERED HABITS

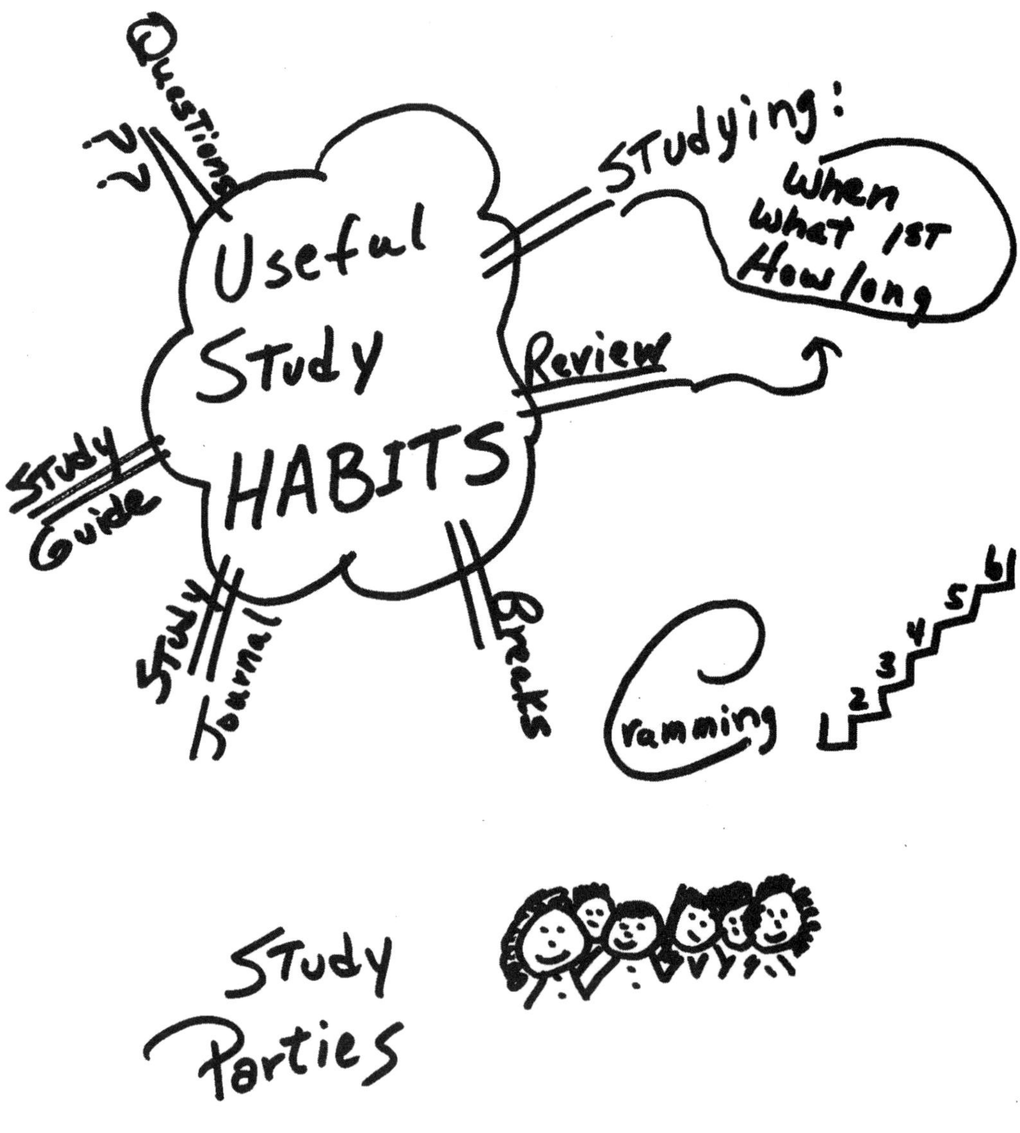

IN THIS CHAPTER

	PAGE
▶ USEFUL STUDY HABITS	115
▶ STUDY PARTIES	135
▶ STUDY TRAPS	138

Sneak Previews

There are MANY ways to learn –

USEFUL study habits can help you do it better, especially if you avoid study traps.

Save time & Remember more.

Studying isn't a spectator sport. But it's OK to take breaks.

There's a method to Cramming Madness.

Party on, Dudes – STUDY Parties!

V.I.P.
Very Important Point

There are study habits and there are *study habits....*

AND...some study habits are useful and some aren't.

What is that supposed to mean?

Yeah. It doesn't make much sense...

Read on. It's easier than it sounds.

USEFUL STUDY HABITS

How often have you sat down to study, or begun an assignment with something else on your mind?

If you're like most students, it happens a lot. To learn faster and make the most of your study time, develop some useful habits.

KNOWING WHEN TO STUDY (Self *SMART*)

When's the best time to study? That depends on when you can find time and what works for you. The most important thing is to try to study (as much as possible) at a regular time – the same time each day.

Now would be a good time to take a look at some time management suggestions –

Mental Bungee JUMP

To
Chapter 2 in
SMART Studying Handbook 3 –
Extending Your Power

KNOWING HOW LO-O-O-O-O-NG TO STUDY
(Self *SMART*)

RULE OF THUMB:

2 to 3 hours of study per week for each class.

If you have **5 classes**, you can expect to spend **10-15 hours per week** studying.

I don't spend half that much time!

I can't even count the hours – it's too scary.

Use your study ***SMARTS*** – you shouldn't short-change yourself, but don't waste time, either. Get this study 'rite' right!

You may be studying ineffectively.

ANOTHER RULE OF THUMB

Spending lots of time studying doesn't guarantee you'll remember what you've studied.

That's a goofy-sounding rule!

It may sound goofy, but it's true. I'll show you –

Try this math problem...

1 hour studying...
You'll remember what you learned in the 1st ***and last 15 minutes.***

2 hours studying...
You'll remember what you learned in the 1st ***and last 15 minutes.***

It's easy to see that studying twice for one hour is better then studying once for two hours.

That's a no-brainer! I'll study for 30 minutes. That way, I'll remember it all.

Good try. But –

V.I.P.
Very Important Point

It doesn't really matter how long you study, you're still going to lose the middle part.

That's not fair!

Unfortunately, it's true.

The point is –
Studying some each day gives you
more beginnings and endings
(and shorter middles).

KNOWING WHAT TO STUDY FIRST

(Self *SMART*)

FREE ADVICE –
TOO GOOD TO IGNORE

Study difficult (or boring) subjects first.

The temptation is to begin with what you like best. But your energy level is highest when you start. So take advantage of the higher energy and get the most difficult tasks finished right away.

MAKING A STUDY GUIDE
(**Logic**, **Eye**, and **Naturalist** ***SMARTS***)

Make a study guide for every class. Include

✓main ideas
✓vocabulary
✓theories
✓formulas
✓names & dates
✓problem types
(for math & scien

If your teacher does all the work and gives you a study guide, be smart enough to use it.

As you study, check off each item on your guide. Is there anything you don't understand? Are there any points you have trouble remembering?

Go back and review.

KEEPING A STUDY JOURNAL

A Study Journal is a record of your **thoughts, ideas, feelings,** and **hopes** about what you're studying. Record your **mistakes,** too – it's a quick way to start learning from them. Journaling helps you see connections between new knowledge and old.

A Journal gives you the chance to use your

- ▶ **Word *SMARTS*** and **Body *SMARTS*** (by writing)
- ▶ **Logic *SMARTS*** (by looking for ways to connect what you're learning to what you already know)
- ▶ **Self *SMARTS*** (by expressing your feelings [good & bad], and by thinking about what you wrote)
- ▶ **Eye *SMARTS*** (if you include sketches or information maps)
- ▶ **Ear *SMARTS*** (if you read aloud)

When you read your entries, **look for patterns** of how you're using your ***SMARTS***. Then you know what to do again and what to avoid.

HOT TIP

Journals help you be as SMART as you can be – Celebrate that success

DIVIDING AND CONQUERING
(Self *SMART*)

▶ Does the very sight of that fat chapter give you the shivers?

▶ Do you get a headache just thinking about starting that term paper?

The bad news, of course, is it will look just as evil tomorrow.

And the worse news is that 'doing it tomorrow' usually doesn't happen.

HOT TIP

Don't panic –
Instead, divide and conquer.

- Take a careful look at your assignment.
    - Divide the assignments into small steps. Make a list.
        - Be sure each step is truly small – something you can accomplish in a reasonable amount of time.
            - Prioritize the steps – from most to least important.
                - Set a goal of completing the steps one at a time. Then cross them off your list – proof positive that you're making progress.

ASKING QUESTIONS (**Logic** and **Self** ***SMART***)

Story

Kim took a university course with her friend, John, who was very shy. During the first two classes they sat together. But after that John refused to sit with her. She asked so many questions she embarrassed him.

Kim was astonished. Her attitude was – if I don't know, I'll ask. His attitude was – wait, the professor will tell me what I need to know.

Asking questions is a time-honored method of learning. So, when do you ask questions? How about all the time?

That might work for some people, but it's not my style.

Even so, it's not smart to wait and hope the teacher will explain if you really don't understand something!

Whether you're the shy type or someone who's more willing to speak up and risk making a fool of yourself –

ALWAYS ask questions of *yourself* as you study.

- Quiz yourself on the material you're studying.
  - Make notes of points you're not sure you understand – turn them into questions to ask the next day in class.
    - Pretend you're the teacher and create test questions – then be sure to answer them!

TAKING ANOTHER LOOK (All *SMARTS*)

Did you know?

With systematic review –
you can expect to remember **88%** of new knowledge.

Without systematic review –
you can expect to remember **10%.**

All you have to do is a little review.

Review time can be **as little as 5 minutes for a 50 minute class.** Each time you sit down to study, start with a 5–10 minute review. When you're finished studying, take a break for an hour or two, then do another quick review. Review (yet again) –

- after one day,
    - after one week,
        - and after one month.

But it works!

More good news – the more you review, the less time it takes.

HOT TIP

Save time and remember more. Review frequently for short periods.

> **Note:** No matter what subject you're studying, review doesn't mean just staring at the book for an extra five minutes!
> Nor does it mean simply re-reading your notes. When you review you need to use your ***SMARTS*** **–**

- Re-organize your notes into information maps. (**Eye *SMART***)

- Make an inventory of the main ideas in your notes.
  (**Naturalist *SMART***)

- Make up test questions based on your notes.
  (**Word *SMART***)

- ✏ Talk aloud to yourself; chant or sing the information.
  (**Ear *SMART***)
- ✏ Use a mnemonic device – or two or three.
  (**Word, Ear, Logic *SMARTS***)
- ✏ Teach someone; or call a friend and quiz each other.
  (**People *SMART***)
- ✏ Dance, march, bounce a ball, or just pace.
  (**Body *SMART***)

For ideas –

Mental Bungee JUMP
To
Chapter 4 in this handbook
And
Chapter 3 in ***SMART*** Studying Handbook 2 –
Using Your Power Base

HOT TIP

Review doesn't have to be boring.

TAKING A BREAK (Body *SMART*)

I need a break! But I bet breaks are forbidden, right?

Not at all! Breaks are important – you should take one at least every ninety minutes.

BUT…

V.I.P.
Very Important Point

A break means just that:
***a break* – a short pause in studying.**

▶ **It's NOT** the time to phone your best friend or see what's on TV.

▶ **It IS** the time to get up and move around.

Drink some milk or water. Nibble on some healthy snacks.

Take a walk.

Play some music. For suggestions –

Get really ambitious and do some exercises.

Call a friend and chat for a while. A SHORT while.

Mental Bungee JUMP

To
Chapter 8 in this handbook

CRAMMING (Not *SMART*)

Cramming isn't smart, but let's face it–
sometimes you just have to.

FREE ADVICE -
TOO GOOD TO IGNORE

Don't get in this situation!

Too late! So
what can I do?

First, be realistic. Limit cramming sessions to no more than 30 minutes. Take a five-minute break, then study again.

Second, gear your studying to the kind of test you'll be taking –

- If it's going to be an essay test, focus on remembering how information is related.
- If it will be an objective test, work on remembering facts and details.

Third, use a –

'Sensible' Cramming Method

- Start by **organizing**. (Be sure to use all your ***SMARTS***)
  - Get to the **bare essentials**. Make an **outline**. **Prioritize** key concepts and **focus** on them.
    - Use **mnemonics** to make **memorizing** easier.
      - On **test day** get up early enough to **review again.**

If you have to pull an all-nighter, get into high gear and use the (semi-) Sensible All-Nighter Plan.

How can pulling an all-nighter ever be even Semi-sensible?

You have to plan ahead. But you can do it in 6 easy steps...

1 – Stock Up – *Got milk?*

Don't eat for the first 3 or 4 hours, then snack every couple of hours to keep up your energy. **Make healthy choices** – fruit, raw veggies, a high-energy bar, maybe a (healthy) oatmeal cookie, an energy drink (avoid caffeine).

2 – Set The Scene

Don't get too comfortable. Dress for success – don't wear your pajamas. Turn on all the lights. Sit at your desk in a straight-backed chair.

3 – Make a Time Table

Plan what you're going to study **every hour**. Write it down.

4 – Reward Yourself

As you finish **each hour**, congratulate yourself with a reward. Eat a cookie, play a favorite song, do a dance or a cheer. Make it **quick**.

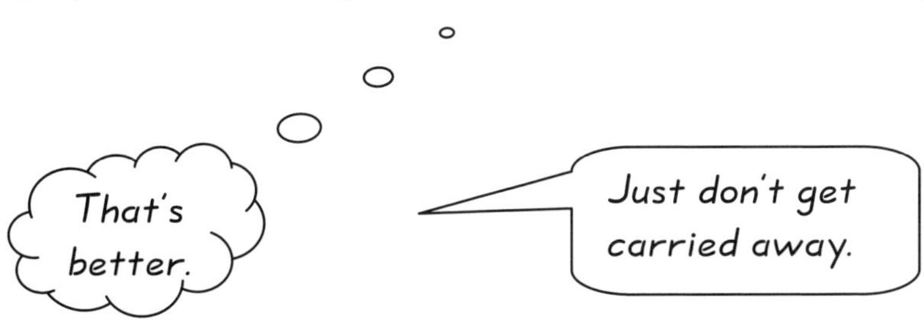

5 – Be Adventuresome!

Don't stress out – think of your all-nighter as an adventure (hopefully, it's not a repeat experience). If you feel anxious, remember to breathe, stand up and give yourself a good all-over shake, then relax all your muscles.

An adventure... Somehow, I've never thought of studying as an adventure before!

6 – Avoid The Bed Trap

Don't even think about your bed!

Stay away from your bed. If you think you don't have any place to study except the bed, think again. Sit on the floor! Never, ever, ever even *sit* on the bed – it's too dangerous!

HOT TIP

If you must cram, do it right.

WARNING! (Read the fine print.) Don't review as you're going in to class to take the test. It's too easy in your haste to make a mistake and confuse yourself.
Also, don't start asking your classmates for help just before the test. They're just as likely as you are to make a mistake due to haste and give you wrong information.

And More fine print! Cramming mostly won't work in math and science courses. Think about it – you couldn't do long division if you didn't know how to add, subtract, and multiply. Many things in both math and science work that way. If you're in a cram situation, you don't have time to start at the beginning and review everything – it's much safer to keep current in these classes and avoid the need for cramming.

STUDY PARTIES

(People *SMART*)

STUDY Party Invitation

When: Tonight
Where: My house
What to bring: Books, notes, outlines, mnemonics, old tests, a smart friend (limit:5-7 people total)

Snacks & music provided.

Study parties are a terrific invention! And a great chance to use all your SMARTS/

- Somebody will know the things you don't.

- What's missing from your notes will be in someone else's.

- Drills are much easier to do with a friend than alone.

- Doing math or science problems with friends may give you strategies you wouldn't have thought of alone.

- Discussing, debating, and questioning stimulates thought and opens your mind. It also forces you to clarify your thinking.

I hope they at least have munchies...

They will.

Note: Study parties are useful even if you're the top student – explaining something to someone else will solidify your own understanding.

And other people appreciate the help.

That's good....It doesn't always happen that way outside of parties.

More fine print! 'Studying' isn't the same as being tutored. Each person needs to come to a study party ready to STUDY. If you haven't done the homework or don't understand anything about the class material, what you need is a tutoring session. Classmates whose intent was to study won't appreciate having to teach you everything.

Three to five people is a good sized study party, but larger groups can work IF everyone is serious about studying.

My best friend is a real funny guy – he's never serious about anything!

Invite him to your regular parties, but let him know study parties are truly for studying.

For information about participating in a group –

Mental Bungee JUMP

To
Chapter 8 in ***SMART*** Studying Handbook 2 –
Using Your Power Base

STUDY TRAPS

There are lots of study traps out there, just waiting to catch you. Have you ever fallen into any of these?

- **"I don't know where to begin."**
- **"I don't have enough time – there's too much to study."**
- **"This stuff is so boring, I can't even stay awake reading it."**
- **"I read it; I understand it; it just doesn't stick with me."**
- **"I knew it a minute ago."**
- **"Cramming before a test helps me keep stuff fresh in my mind."**
- **"I already know this stuff; I don't need to study."**
- **"My study partners aren't available; I can wait till this afternoon or tomorrow or next week."**

These are common traps, but you know better. If there's one that still gets you –

Mental Bungee JUMP

Back to the Appropriate Section of this Chapter

CHAPTER 7
PLUG IN HYPER-SPEED
STUDY SKILLS

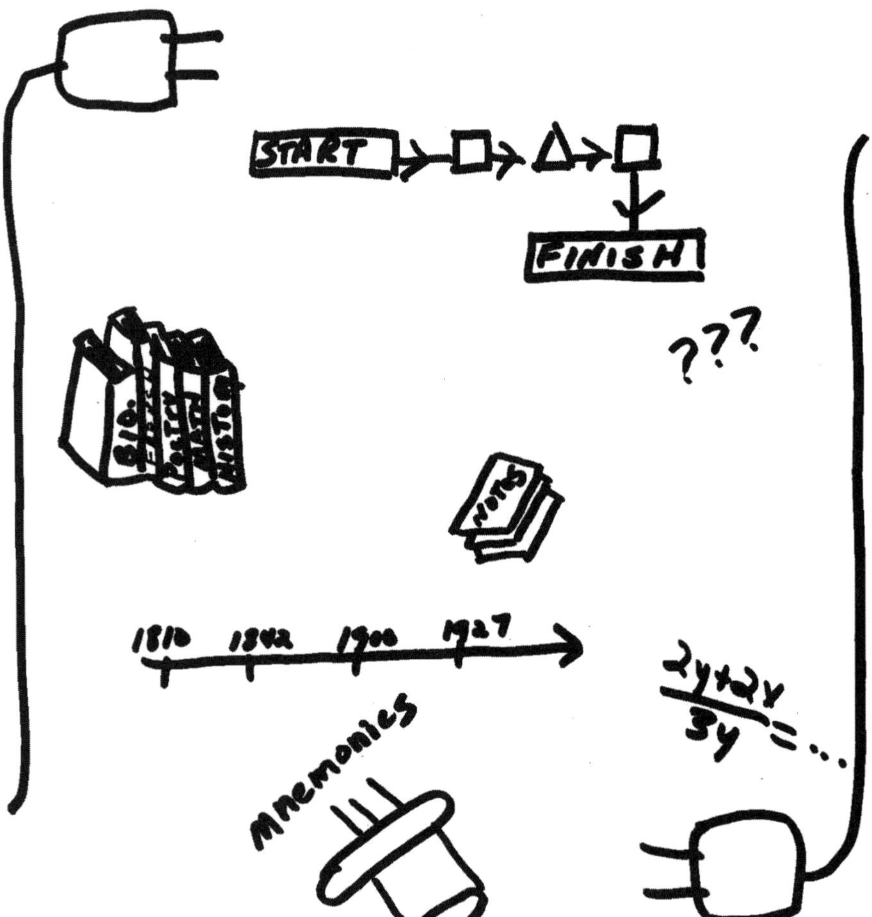

IN THIS CHAPTER

	PAGE
▶STUDY SKILLS	142
▶ ALL SUBJECT PLUG-INS	144
▶ PLUG-INS FOR SPECIAL CIRCUMSTANCES	161

Sneak Previews

There are MANY ways to learn – (study different subjects differently).

Ask questions!

Check books & other references for accuracy.

Flash cards aren't just for 3rd graders.

Mnemonics are magic.

Use special techniques for studying math, science, and foreign languages.

*

STUDY SKILLS

What's skill got to do with studying? Studying's just a lot of hard work, that's all.

Have you ever thought about how to study?

What's to think about? Studying means you just sit down and get to work.

And what does that mean?

What '**skills**' do you need for studying?

And just what does '**get to work studying**' mean?

To see what answers YOU come up with –

Take the –

STUDY SKILLS QUESTIONNAIRE

When I study, I:

____ repeat the information over and over.

____ study on a regular schedule.

____ study in an organized way.

____ create my own mnemonics.

____ draw pictures of the information.

____ take notes on textbook chapters.

____ am serious – take a get-down-to-work attitude.

____ study with a group.

____ talk aloud to myself (or into a tape recorder).

____ teach the material to someone else.

____ summarize my textbook.

____ study differently for different subjects.

There are no right or wrong answers to the Questionnaire. But notice what you didn't mark – what doesn't work for you. The point is to think about how you study.

The following ideas are **POWERFUL** study aids for learning most subjects

ALL SUBJECT PLUG-INS

VOCABULARY

Every subject has its own vocabulary. The more advanced your class is, the more specialized the vocabulary becomes.

Use Word *SMARTS* –

Make a glossary:

Computer terms:

Boot: to start or restart a computer

Path: the route through a file system

Site: the location of a Web page

Vocabulario:

uno = one

dos = two

tres = thr

In science and math, 'ordinary,' 'every-day' words often mean something quite different from their normal English meaning! In science, for example –

Physics Vocabulary

Normal: a line perpendicular to a surface

Accelerate: the rate of change of velocity with respect to time

Velocity: speed **+** direction

V.I.P.
Very Important Point

It's helpful to think of science as a foreign language!

In science, a word often stands for an entire complex concept, and what you are learning when you learn the word is the *concept*. The subtle difference between the usual meaning and the physics meaning can be very confusing. So, without a knowledge of the terms and phrases (the jargon) of whatever discipline you're studying, you'll be lost.

HOT TIP

Learn the language.

TEXTBOOK READING

Reading a textbook isn't quite the same as reading a novel.

Uh duh!

Reading textbooks is like reading the original Hunchback of Notre Dame instead of the comic book version – they tell the same story, but the comic book is easier than the original to understand.

For suggestions on how to speed up your textbook reading –

Mental Bungee JUMP

To

Chapter 2 in ***SMART*** Studying Handbook 2 – *Using Your Power Base*

MATH AND SCIENCE TEXTBOOKS

When reading math textbooks, STOP if you don't understand everything on each page. Don't skip over things you don't understand. Each page builds on the page before. If you don't understand one step, you won't be able to take the next one. Think about what you're reading. Work out any problems included in the text, or study the example problems. If you have trouble understanding the text, find a different one that you can understand.

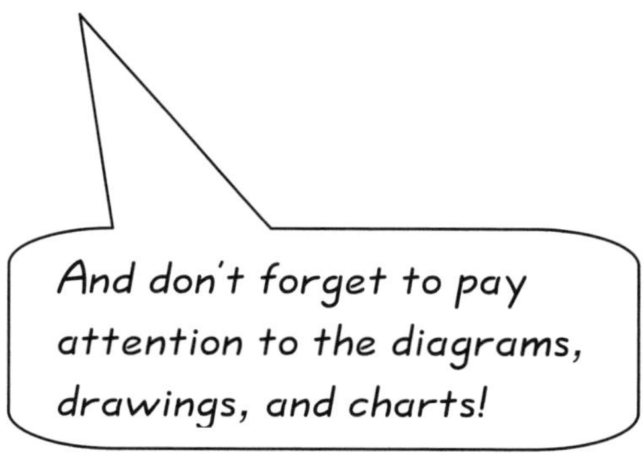

USING ILLUSTRATIONS, CHARTS, & DIAGRAMS
(Eye *SMARTS*)

Don't!!
Pay attention – study them! Sometimes a picture really is worth 1000 words. Diagrams often summarize whole sections of a chapter.

QUESTION ASKING (**Word, Logic, People, Naturalist**, and **Ear *SMARTS***)

WHO –

discovered…?
said…?
tried…?
founded…:
persuaded…?
was responsible for…?
helped…?
decided…?
solved…?
invented…?
was first to…?

WHERE –

is…?
was…?
were…?
could you find…?
is it possible to…?
was …discovered?
will… lead?

WHAT –
happened?
were the effects of…?
were the roles of…
are some ways to…?
caused…?

HOW –
can you tell if…?
does…work?
did…happen?
is…different from…?
are…and… the same?
did…influence...?

WHEN –
did…live?
was…invented?
does…matter?
will…happen?
should we…?

WHY–
did… happen?
is…important?
should…be changed?
couldn't someone…?
do we need…?
is it that…?
not…?

> **A Note about "Who?" questions –**
> Some historical figures were eventful.
> Others were event-making.

▶ Important events would have occurred with or without **eventful people.**

The Industrial Revolution would have occurred no matter who was head of government, so England's Queen Victoria is considered an eventful person with respect to the industrial revolution.

▶ Event-making people, however, significantly affect history.

Some events happened largely because of an event-making person – Without Hitler, the Holocaust would not have happened.

V.I.P.
Very Important Point

When your purpose is studying, it's important to ask questions you have a chance of answering.

Why? I've always been told, 'The only bad question is the one you don't ask!'

True. But consider: "Why is the sky blue?" is an unanswerable question for a six-year-old, but isn't beyond the research capability of a general physics student.

I see what you mean.

HOT TIP

Asking questions is the fastest, most powerful way to learn.

ACCURACY CHECK

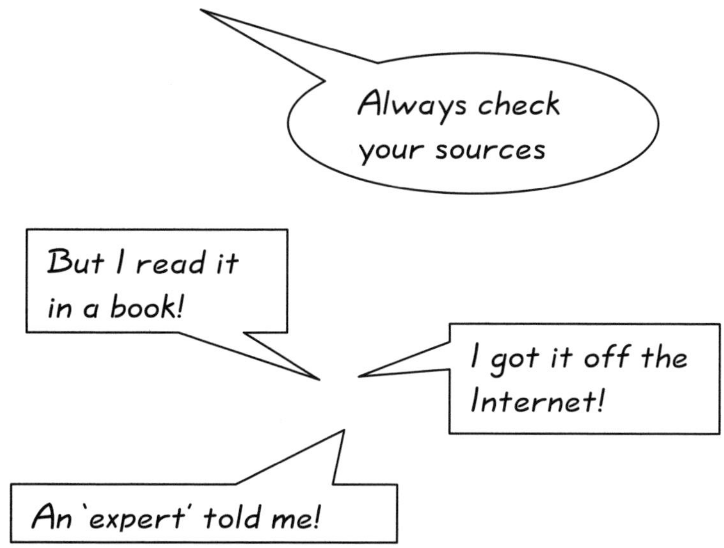

It doesn't matter. Check your sources!

Make a habit of thinking of 'facts' as hypotheses. Even so-called geographical 'facts' in respected sources can be in error. It's possible to discover several 'facts' concerning the length of the Mississippi River.

And as for history – it's written by historians. Historians are people. People have opinions, biases, blind sides, and axes to grind. Sometimes they make honest mistakes.

So don't dilute your power – check your sources. Ask:

- What evidence exists to support your 'facts'?
  - Are there contradictions in the evidence?
    - Is a biased viewpoint likely?

HOT TIP

Not all 'facts' are created equal.

FLOW CHARTS

Flow charts are a way of putting information into pictures. They use **Logic, Eye,** and **Naturalist *SMARTS*** to organize information and show :

- sequences and processes.
  - cause and effect relationships.
    - chronological information.

To be useful, flow charts must be clear. Ask yourself questions – the more, the better. For example –

- What's the first thing that happened? or
  Who did it?

- What's the next thing that happened? or
  Who was affected?

- What were the results? and
  What happened next?

Simplicity is the key.

HOW TO DO IT IN 5 EASY STEPS

- describe the process (or hierarchy or series of events) to be charted;
  - begin with a 'trigger' event (or head honcho);
    - note each successive action (or person) concisely and clearly;
      - stay with the main flow (exclude details); and
        - follow the process (or hierarchy or events) through to a useful (or logical) conclusion.

Every flow chart has:

- a START and STOP symbol.
  - a top–to–bottom sequence flow (loops can flow back to an entry point).
    - arrow-heads on connectors where flow direction may not be obvious.

Draw only one flow chart per page and complete the chart on the page – don't finish it on another page.

The most commonly used flow chart symbols are:

Used to show the beginning and end of a sequence

Gives instructions to follow

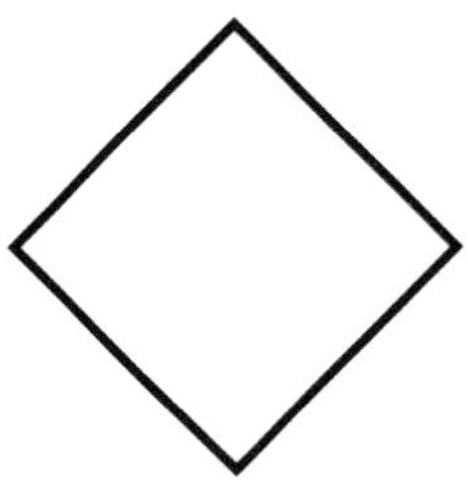

These are decision boxes which contain yes or no questions

The symbols are joined together by directional arrows. A simple example:

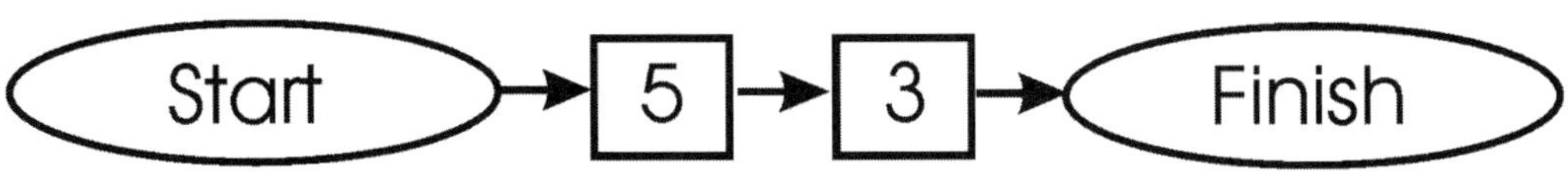

To use the above chart, think of a number and follow the chart. For example, if you think of the number 2, you would:

Add 5 to 2 to get 7;
then multiply 7 by 3 to get 21
This means when you put 2 in,
you get 21 out.

TIME LINES

*(***Logic/Number** and **Eye** ***SMARTS****)*

A time line represents the flow of time in intervals of hours, weeks, months, years, decades, centuries – you choose. It doesn't matter if you draw the time line horizontally or vertically.

Time lines give you the power to organize dates, events, and people into an easily remembered framework. When you study the time line,

- relate the dates to events you're familiar with –
  - or relate events to one another

Gandalf arrived BEFORE Bilbo's birthday party.

The electric dental drill was patented 10 years AFTER the U.S. Civil War.

Queen Victoria died, Teddy Roosevelt became the 26th President, and x-rays were discovered—all in 1901.

BRAINSTORMING

(**People, Self**, and **Word** ***SMARTS***)

Brainstorming can be done alone or in a group – it works well either way.

Here are a few useful rules:

- **Generate** as many **ideas** as **fast** as possible.
- **Wild, off-beat** ideas are best.
- **No criticism** is allowed.
- **Hitchhike** – combine (or even force) ideas together.

FLASH CARDS (All *SMARTS*)

Flash cards are for people who want to practice or rehearse what they're studying.

Depending on HOW you use them, flash cards can be **Eye, Ear, People, Word, Naturalist**, or **Self *SMART***.

English & History Flash Cards:

- vocabulary
- dates
- time periods
- important people & their contributions
- cause/effect
- quotations

Math & Science Flash Cards:

- vocabulary/terms
- concepts
- numbers
- symbols
- formulas
- illustrations
- names & dates

Foreign Language Flash Cards:

- vocabulary
- grammatical forms
- verb conjugations
- pronoun declensions
- singular and plural forms of nouns
- irregular verbs

HOT TIP

Color code your foreign language flash cards to show masculine, feminine, and neutral nouns.

MNEMONICS

Panic! Panic!
I need help – I'll never be able to remember all 13 characters in 'Twelfth Night'!

THAT'S WHAT MNEMONICS ARE FOR

Mnemonics are memory games –
reminders, hints, prompts,& nudges
rhymes, jingles, stories, & puzzles

I'll believe it works when I see it.

That's fair. To see it –

Mental Bungee JUMP
To
Chapter 5 in this handbook

PLUG-INS FOR SPECIAL CIRCUMSTANCES*

* Math, Science, & Foreign Languages

MATH (Logic/Number *SMARTS*)

PROBLEM SOLVING

These problems are hard – you can't solve them in one step!

No, but you can solve them one step at a time…break each problem into smaller pieces before you start.

- Start with problems you already know how to solve.

  - Work just one type of problem at a time.

    - Work problems until you understand them, not just until you get the right answer for the homework. Aim to solve as much of the problem as possible before consulting any other sources.

      - Use your calculator as a tool – not as a substitute for your own logic. Use it later rather than sooner when solving a problem.

Problem solving strategies:

- solve a simpler related problem
- use one or more variables
- look for a formula
- complete a table
- draw a picture or diagram
- look for a pattern
- guess, then test
- consider a special case
- work backward

Story

When my nine-year-old son asked for help in solving a word problem that began, 'A train left the station…' my throat went dry, my stomach tied itself in knots, and I started to feel faint! I had to give myself a no-nonsense lecture on the idiocy of a grown woman having a panic attack over fourth-grade math before I could even begin to help – and even then, it wasn't easy.

FREE ADVICE - YOU CAN'T AFFORD TO IGNORE

Re-program your thinking.

- Delete thoughts like *'I can't do word problems.'*
  - Think of story problems as 'applied problems.' After all, the whole point in solving them is to give you an idea of how math helps solve real-world (applied) problems.

Remember – one step at a time!

1. Read the problem carefully. Read it again. Make sure you fully understand what the problem is asking.

2. Think about the problem using math terminology.

> *That means think about terms like 'area,' 'logarithm,' 'least common denominator.' Using math terms helps you know what needs to be done.*

2½. Now you're ready to figure out what formulas or math facts you need to use. Sometimes it's useful to make diagrams, charts, or drawings to help visualize the problem.

3. State the problem as a mathematical equation or formula.

4. Do the math. (Believe it or not, this is usually the easy part!)

5. Convert the answer back to words.

6. Read the problem again to make sure you've solved the right problem. (If the question was *'How much change should Johnny get?'* and your answer is *'Johnny spent a total of $150.55'* you haven't solved the right problem even if you're correct about how much he spent.)

7. Check your answer. Make sure it makes sense (trains don't travel 4,000 miles per hour; cans of paint cover more than 4 square feet). Also double check for careless arithmetic errors.

MORE FREE ADVICE –

Avoid Careless Errors

- ✓ Do practice drills of basic math facts –addition, subtraction, multiplication tables – if necessary.
- ✓ Take your time. Haste often truly does make waste.
- ✓ Don't skip the "Check your answer" step. Double-check plus & minus signs.

HOT TIP

Math skills are important in science. BUT – Formulas are just shorthand symbols for principles.

Another HOT TIP

To prevent costly mistakes, make sure you understand the scientific principle BEFORE you use a formula.

SCIENCE
(Logic/Number, Word, Ear, Body, Naturalist, & People *SMARTS*)

LABS

- Write your report as soon as possible after doing the lab.
  - Presentation counts – tidy graphs, colored & labeled illustrations, and legible writing help make the grade.
    - Keep a separate notebook for lab materials.

A 3 ring binder with pockets for handouts and study aids works well.

Use dividers to separate different labs.

PROBLEM SOLVING:

Read the problem carefully – twice. Ask yourself: What's the problem about?

→ Ask: What am I asked to find? Get rid of any extra details you don't need – reduce the problem to its essentials.

→ Draw and label a suitable diagram

→ Ask: What information am I to use? List the given quantities and the required quantities.

→ Ask yourself: What principles apply? Write out some relevant principles (usually in mathematical form).

→ Ask: What do I know about similar problems? and How can I apply what I know to solving this problem? Analyze the problem, think about it, look for relationships between the various factors

→ Do the math. Note that frequently you won't want a numerical solution – only an algebraic one. Get used to it.

→ Check your answer. Ask: Does my solution make sense

→ Check your answer with your text book. If you didn't get it right, review the problem and try again. Even if you were right, review the problem.

HOT TIP

Don't spend too much time on any one problem.

If you haven't made any progress after 15 minutes, you're probably missing something.

Go on to other problems, and come back to the hard ones when you've had a bit more practice.

FOREIGN LANGUAGES

(**Word** and **Ear** ***SMARTS***)

Speak up in class. At the very least, if you have trouble speaking up, think the words to yourself when others are called on to speak.

But it's best if you can let yourself be spontaneous.

Take risks – you'll learn faster and have more fun, too.

How?

V.I.P.
Very Important Point

Practice is the key.

Join language clubs, watch Foreign TV, listen to foreign radio, read a foreign newspaper or magazine. Or study out loud with a friend or with a native speaker. (**Use Ear, Word, Self,** and **People *SMARTS***)

REVIEW (Use **ALL *SMARTS***)

Reviewing often is even more important for Math, Science and Foreign Languages than for other subjects.

✏ **Don't get behind.** Manage your time so you stay on top of the work.

- ▶ Every lesson builds on the ones before. If you don't understand Chapter 4, you probably won't understand Chapters Five or Six.

- ▶ Falling a day behind puts you at a disadvantage.

- ▶ Falling a week behind puts you in deep trouble.

- ▶ And cramming the night before tests spells disaster!

- ▶ Studying for small amounts of time is more effective than trying to study a lot all at once. Sometimes your understanding is increased by just letting it sit for a day and then coming back to it.

✏ **Don't memorize** anything you don't understand.

✏ **Get help** – do whatever it takes, but make sure you do understand.

CHAPTER 8

TURN ON THE MUSIC

IN THIS CHAPTER

	PAGE
▶ THE POWER OF MUSIC	173
▶ A SOUND SOLUTION	176
▶ MUSIC CHOICE IDEAS	181
▶ SONGS AND RAPS	186

Sneak Previews

Music exerts powerful influences.

There are MANY different types of music that will help you study.

The key is discovering what music works best for you.

Don't over-use music during study periods.

Do use a change of music during study breaks.

THE *POWER OF* MUSIC

Music affects our bodies and brains in a variety of ways. It can make us feel frightened, anxious, excited, joyful – in general, music heightens our sense of awareness. Think about the last movie you saw. Imagine it without music. How would you know something scary was going to happen without the sinister music to clue you in? The next time you watch a movie, pay attention to the music and the way it's used.

> When you add the power of music to the way emotions affect everything we do, it's easy to see the connection between music and learning.

HOT TIP

Your brain loves to learn with music.

EFFECT ON LEARNING

Theory:*

The sound wave frequencies in Baroque music (1700's – Mozart's general time period) stimulate your brain so much that it's possible for you to learn up to five times faster than if you studied without music.

* Don Campbell, *The Mozart Effect*

That sure adds speed & power to your learning!

▶ While the 'Mozart effect' hasn't been definitely proven, many students find that playing the right kind of background music while they study helps in many ways – (music can activate your **Ear *SMARTS***).

▶ You learn faster.

▶ You're more creative

AND

▶ You get better grades.

Background music gets into your memory – even if you aren't really paying attention to it. That helps you remember whatever you WERE paying attention to!

MINOR PROBLEM:

It seems to work best when the same music is used for study and recall, such as in test taking.

Would your teachers let you play a tape of your study music while taking a test?

That doesn't seem very likely!

Maybe if I listen to my study music enough I can play the tape mentally for myself...

A SOUND SOLUTION

BEFORE YOU STUDY

I suppose it makes sense to choose study music I like . . .

But I like different music at different time . . . How I feel always influences what music I choose.

So, when you choose music for studying, consider your mood and how alert you are in addition to what you like.

Find out what kind of music can get you going if you aren't in the mood to study.

- If you feel stressed – choose calm, soothing music. Sit quietly; breathe deeply.

- If you feel bored or drowsy – try a more active approach. Choose upbeat, active music (maybe a Sousa march or rock music). You should be ready to study in a few minutes.

And remember, it only makes sense to choose music you enjoy.

HOT TIP

The key to facilitating learning is to discover what kind of music works for you.

WHILE YOU STUDY

FREE ADVICE – TOO GOOD TO IGNORE

Use Baroque music unless you really hate it.

Even if you think you hate it, you should give it a try.

Why bother?

Baroque music works for lots of people as a study aid even if it isn't their favorite music to listen to on a regular basis.

There's even a research study about 12-year-olds who listened to Baroque music when they studied – not because they liked it, but because it worked!

What if I really do hate Baroque music?

Don't sweat it. Experiment with another type.

Try classical guitar music. Or Gregorian chants. Or New Age music. Or some mellow jazz. Or music with sounds of nature included. Or . . .

ALTERNATIVELY...

You don't have to listen to music while you study.

- Maybe you're accustomed to studying 'with no distractions' – that's OK. Just turn the music off once you're ready to study.

SOUND BREAKS

HOT TIP

Regular study breaks are a must – they help you re-focus.

10 minutes – plus or minus a few – is an ideal break period.

And 'Break Time' is great time to let music work some magic for you!

- Turn on more (or different) music.
  - Choose exciting music to play during your break to wake you up and re-energize your brain.
    - Go back to your 'study' music when your break is over.

TOO MUCH, TOO LOUD, TOO SOFT?

- Don't play music continuously while you study – it can lose its effect.

  - Pay attention to the volume – that's important, too.

    - Too loud can be distracting – even irritating. and 'too loud' isn't necessarily very loud at all when you're trying to concentrate on something else.

      - Too soft won't work, either.

Experiment to get it right for you.

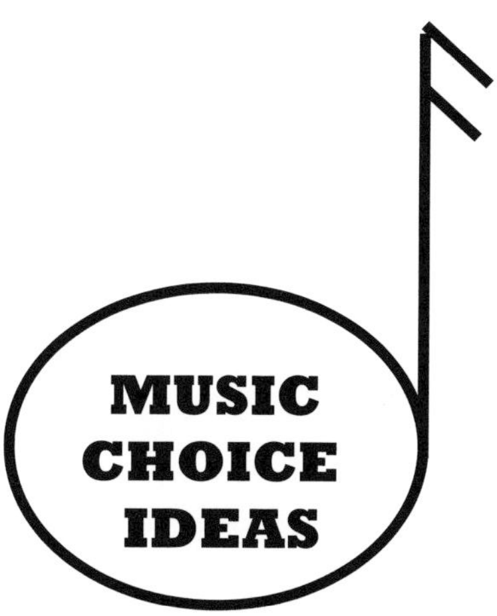

Besides your own personal favorites, here are some specific suggestions for good study music.

BAROQUE COMPOSERS (1660 - 1750)

Baroque music often has three movements – fast-slow-fast.

The slow – Largo – movements are the best for study music.

Bach, J.S. *Brandenburg Concertos 1-6.*

Baroque Guitar, played by Julian Bream.

Baroque Horn Concertos, played by Barry Tuckwell.

Handel, George Frederick. *Water Music.*

Pachelbel, Johann. *Canon.*

Vivladi, Antonio. *The Four Seasons.*
Cello Concertos.

CLASSICAL AND ROMANTIC COMPOSERS (1770- 1885)

Beethoven, Ludwig.

Cello Sonatas.

Complete Chamber Music for Flute.

Symphony #6 – Pastoral.'

Chopin, Frederic. *Piano Concertos, Nos. 1 &2.*

Dvorak, Antonin. *Symphony No.9 "From the New World."*

Haydn, Joseph. *Cello Concertos.*

Mozart, Amadeus. *Horn Concertos.*

MUSIC FOR RELAXATION

If you're tired or stressed, or if you've been concentrating for a long time, try some of the following suggestions.

All you have to do is sit back and listen for 5-10 minutes and you'll feel rejuvenated.

Campbell, Don. *Crystal Rainbows*.

Campbell, Don. *Runes* (deep relaxation)

Debussy, Claude. *Afternoon of a Fawn*

Dexter, Ron. *Golden Voyage*. Awakening Productions, 4132 Tuller Ave., Culver City, CA 90230

Eno, Brian. *The Pearl.*

Gardner, Kay. *Rainbow Path.*

Goldman, Jonathan. *Dolphin Dreams.* (deep relaxation)

Halpern, Steven. *Dawn*.

Halpern, Steven. *Spectrum Suite.*

Kobialka, Daniel. *Timeless Motion.*

Lind Institute. *Relax with the Classics.* (Adagio)

Lind Institute. *Relax with the Classics.* (Largo)

Robertson, Kim. *Wind Shadows*. (Celtic harp) Sakura. Artist: Jean-Pierre Rampal and Lily Laskine. Columiba M-34568. (This is music for flute and harp based on Japanese melodies.)

MUSIC FOR CONCENTRATION

If you're having trouble concentrating, try playing one of the following selections softly in the background.

Campbell, Don. *Cosmic Classics.*

Campbell, Don. *Crystal Meditations.*

Gregorian chant.

Lanz, David. *Nightfall.*

Lind Institute . *Relax with the Classics* (Andante).

Mozart, W. A. *C Major Piano Concerto* (Elvira Madigan theme).

Rainer, John . *Songs of the Indian Flute.*

Winston, George. *December.*

Winter, Paul. *Sunsinger.*

MUSIC FOR SOUND BREAKS

If you've been studying for a long time and are sleepy, you need some active, wake-up kind of music for your break. If you've become tense and are having difficulty concentrating, then music which helps you relax would be great.

Try alternating music for relaxation with music for active listening.

Bach, J.S. *Well-Tempered Klavier.*

The Cambridge Busters. *Not Live from New York*

Capelli, Glenn, *Attitude Song*

Born To Teach Song

Crayon Song

It's My Choice Song

My Magic Brain Song

Dances of the Court and Villages of the XVI Century, (Played on old instrument on ODYSSEY 34617).

Flashdance. Theme

Handel, George Frederick. *Royal Fireworks Suite*

Highstein, Max. *Touch the Sky.*

Jensen, Eric. *Music Magic* (a collection of sound cues)

Lynch, Ray. *Deep Breakfast.*

Mannheim Steamroller. *Saving the Wildlife.*

Mozart, W.A. *Symphony in D Major*

Ormandy, Eugene. *Fireworks.*

Soundtrack from *The Sting.*

Sousa, John Phillip. Marches.

Tomita. *Cosmos.*

Tomita. *Snowflakes Are Dancing.*

Tchaikovsky, Peter Illyich. *Piano Concert #1 in B MInor*

Winter, Paul. *Earthbeat.*

Yanni. *Keys to Imagination.*

Another way to use music while you study is to make your own. The melody and rhythm of songs reinforce learning. Give it a try – it's a terrific way to learn! Make up your own songs. Or sing your lessons to a well-known simple melody like *Mary Had a Little Lamb* or *Twinkle, Twinkle Little Star.* It's fun, and you'll remember a lot more than if you just repeated the information ten or twenty boring times.

Raps are great learning tools, too, because of the beat. They work for just about everyone, but they're especially useful for people who learn best by using their **Ear *SMARTS***. Create your own raps using information you want to remember. Say them aloud to a beat. You'll be surprised at how fast you'll remember them. Even a shopping list can be more easily recalled if put into rap form. Try it and see how it works for you.

INDEX

A

accuracy check 153
activity-lack of 63
acronyms 101
acrostics 102
active learner 82
alphabetizing lists 100
association–
  memory 91-93
attitude 33-46

B

baroque composers 182
body SMART 13,24,27,29, 61,62,87,111,121,128,129,166
brainstorming 158
breaks-study 50,172
bungee jumping 9-13

C

celebrate 31,32
chants 61, 87, 105, 128, 184
charts 148,154-56, 164
chunking 96,97
classical and romantic
  composers 182
concentration quick
  fixes 72,73
  see also music for
  concentration 184
coping strategies–
  distractions 53-71
  9-1-1 coping
  strategy 72
cramming 131-134,139

D

daydreaming 70,83
diagrams 148,149,164
distractions
  external 54-59
    heavy class load 59
    location 54-56
    noise 57
    visual 58
  internal 60-71
    day-dreaming 70
    hunger 66
    lack of activity 63
    lack of motivation 68,69
    lack of sleep 64,65
    repeating thoughts,
      jingles, songs 62
    stress 71
    vision problems 66,67
    wandering mind 60,61
    worry 71

E

ear SMART 23,26,45,57 62,86,105,111,121,128, 149,159,166,168,169,174,186
external distractions 54-59
eye SMART 22,23,29,58 67,84,111,120,121, 127,148,154,157,159

F

flash cards 158,159
flow charts 154-156
focus ability 49-52
foreign languages 23, 159, 161,168,169
functional memory 81

H

habits, *see* study habits 114-134
heavy class load 59
hearing 45,46,57
hot tips 8
how long to study 73
how's your focus ability
  questionnaire 51
hunger 66

I

'I don't know' voice 41
illustrations 148
information maps 5,8,15,33, 47,74,112,121,127,140,171

K

Kaizen 37-39

L

labs 166
law of vividness 93,94
link and story
  mnemonic method 106
listening 45,46
location distractions
  analysis questionnaire 55
logic/number SMART 21,22,29, 108,111,157,161,166
logic SMART 103,120, 121,124,128,149,154
long-term memory 80,81
lumpy pancakes 44

M

many kinds of SMARTS 19
math
  problem solving 161-165
  textbooks 148
memory
  functional 81
  long-term 80,81
  myths 79
  recognition 81
  short-term 96,97
mental bungee jumps 9-13
mnemonic methods 97-111
  acronyms 101
  acrostics 102
  alphabetizing lists 100,101
  chants, raps and songs 105
  link and story 106,107
  number rhyme 108-110
  thinking around it 103,104
motivation-lack of 68,69
movement 63,87,103
music 171-186
  baroque composers 182
  classical /romantic
    composers 182
  effect on learning 174
  for concentration 184
  for relaxation 183
  for sound breaks 184,185
  songs and raps 105,186
  sound breaks 180
  using
    before studying 176,177
    while studying 178,179

N

9-1-1 coping strategies 72
naturalist SMART 25,29,84, 100,111,120,127, 149,154,159,166
'no' voice 41
Noise 57
number rhyme mnemonic
  method 108
number SMART 21,22,29
  108,111,161

P

people SMART 24,27,29 56,111,128,135, 149,158,159,166,169
practice 75,88-90 95, 169
problem solving
  process 163-167
  strategies
    math 161-165
    science 166-168

Q

question asking 124,125, 149-152
questionnaires
  how's your focus ability? 51
  location distractions
    analysis 55
  study skills 143
  what kinds of SMART? 20

R

raps 105,186
recognition memory 81
repeating
  jingles 62
  songs 62
  thoughts 62
repetition 88
review 30,31,70, 120,126-128,132,135,169

S

science
  labs 166
  problem solving 167,168
  textbooks 148
self SMART 25,29,30, 42,54,65,111,115,116,119, 121,122,124,158,159,169
self-talk 40-42
short term memory 80,96
sleep – lack of 64
SMARTS 19-30
songs 62,105,186
sound breaks 180
speaking 86
speaking aloud 86
stress 71,134, 177,183
study skills
  breaks-sound 180
  breaks-study 50,70,129
  guides 120
  habits 115-134
    how long to study 50,73,116-118,184
    what to study first 119-123
    when to study 115
  journals 120
  myths 79
  parties 135-137
  questionnaire 143
  textbook reading 147
  traps 138,139
  vocabulary 144-146

T

textbook reading 147
thinking around it mnemonic method 103,104
time
  lines 157
  tracking 50

V

visual distractions 58
visualization 84-86
vision problems 66,67
vocabulary 144-146

W

wandering mind 60,61
what kind of SMARTS questionnaire 20
what to study first 119-123
when to study 115
word SMART 21,43,100-102, 106,111,121,127,128, 145,149,158,159,166,168,169
worry 71
writing 87

Y

'yes' voice 41

The SMART Studying Series

The Power of Knowledge – Knowing How to Best Study to Maximize Potential and Boost Achievement

- Easy-to-understand resource explaining ***how people learn.***
- Terrific visual format for this century's ***visual learners.***
- Outstanding Handbook for introducing awareness of ***Learning Styles*** and ***Study Skills and Habits.***
- Start any time with any book and in any chapter of the book.
- Don't JUST study more or longer. Learn different ways – when, where, and how to study – in order to maximize learning.
- Maximize potential and raise achievement levels. Learn how to take advantage of ALL your ***SMARTS.***

Alone the books are excellent . . . Together, the series is DYNAMITE!

CLC0395	Smart Studying Handbook **1** ***Turning on SMART Power***
CLC0398	Handbook 1 Teacher Edition
CLC0396	Smart Studying Handbook **2** ***Using Your Power Base***
CLC0399	Handbook 2 Teacher Edition
CLC0397	Smart Studying Handbook **3** ***Extending Your Power***
CLC0400	Handbook 3 Teacher Edition

The Teacher Editions include content background, chapter directions, additional student activities, assessment information, and resources.

Available from
Pieces of Learning
1-800-729-5137
www.piecesoflearning.com